The
LAWS
of
SECRET

IRH PRESS

BOOKS

IRH PRESS

New York

ISBN 13: 978-1-942125-81-5

ISBN 10: 1-942125-81-X

Printed in Japan

First Edition

Second Printing

The
LAWS
of
SECRET

Awaken to This New World
and Change Your Life

Ryuho Okawa

IRH Press

Contents

CHAPTER ONE

The Secret World of Religion

Unveiling the Truth about This World and the Afterworld

6 Ways to Deal with Malicious Spirits and Devils

CHAPTER THREE

The Condition of the Real Exorcist

The Spiritual Initiation on Exorcism

1 The Essence of Exorcists

2 The Conditions for Humans to Survive and the Conditions for the Devils to Attack

3 The Targets the Devils Continuously Attack until the End: The Desire for Fame and Jealousy

CHAPTER FOUR

The Right Way to Conquer the Devils
Spiritual Power to Make the World Brighter

CHAPTER FIVE

Creation from Faith

Secrets to Overcoming the Crisis Humanity Faces

4 Build a Pillar of Faith in You and Realize a Prosperous Future

Afterword 223

Preface

With the advancement of science, people say there is nothing that cannot be explained in this modern civilization, but how can that be true? Our lives are full of the unknown.

I want you to awaken more and more to the wonders of living in this world as humans.

This book is full of mysterious episodes and experiences. Many people live every day without being aware of mysterious phenomena, but to the spiritual eyes of a religious leader, the world is truly a brighter place that is guided by another set of rules.

This book shall give you a new view of the world and new guiding principles to live by. When *The Laws of Secret* becomes common knowledge to you, this world will be more beautiful and be filled with delight. And you will surely be thankful for the mystical truth that God's love has been letting you live.

Ryuho Okawa
Master & CEO of Happy Science Group
December 2020

CHAPTER ONE

The Secret World of Religion

Unveiling the Truth about This World and the Afterworld

Originally recorded in Japanese on February 2, 2020, at the Special Lecture Hall of Happy Science in Japan, and later translated into English.

1

How This World Appears from the True World

Academic studies have become an impediment to the Truth

In this chapter, I would like to talk about what I have felt and thought with a foothold in the True World rather than in the earthly ways of life. Academic studies that were introduced to Japan at the end of the 19th century contain some useful subjects such as technical studies, including math and science, and other practical studies, but otherwise, they are completely futile in clarifying the world of Truth or the mystical world taught by religions. They are not only futile but also harmful in a sense. Whereas the purpose of learning must be the pursuit of the Truth, academic studies have become more of a hindrance to the Truth.

To be blunt, these studies are just a pile of junk from the perspective of Buddha's Truth or the True World. This pile of junk can certainly be "sorted" by similarity and "compressed" into something different. But even if it is possible to modify the studies through earthly efforts, junk is still junk; no matter how much they are restructured, they are nothing but an impediment to the Truth.

People's minds are full of such futile knowledge, so even if they experience a spiritual phenomenon, they cannot openheartedly see it as such and end up denying it or becoming skeptical of it. This has become a norm, so there are far fewer people who claim to have had spiritual experiences today than there were in the old days. People actually do have such experiences, but they choose to deny them based on materialistic thinking. So, in most cases, they end up not recognizing them as spiritual experiences.

Most horror movies are unrealistic

On the other hand, in the world of film, both Japanese and foreign horror movies are full of nonsensical scenes from the perspective of someone like me who has had many spiritual experiences. There are mountains of scenes that make me want to say, "There is no way such things can happen in real life!" I think these movies are created based only on imagination.

It may be better for such movies to exist than not having anything related to spiritual phenomena, but these movies are focused on appealing to the human emotion of fear. It appears as if the moviemakers are aiming to amplify people's fear and trying to induce a frightening experience similar to that of riding a roller coaster. They probably want to establish horror as a form of entertainment. So their horror movies are merely an extension of the haunted houses in amusement parks.

I once watched an American horror movie called *The Fog*. The movie was about mariners, who had been murdered by some residents of an island 100 years earlier, appearing from a phantom ship on a foggy day and attacking the island. As expected, the mariners who returned to attack the residents were ghosts. After watching it, I had the impression that some scenes were far too extreme and were depicted just to scare the audience. It apparently earned first place on the opening weekend, but I would say it was more like a B movie.

The ghosts of the mariners that appeared from the phantom ship all had legs. Because the dead are buried according to the customs of Western society, ghosts are portrayed as zombies who come back to life and rise from the grave. That is why these "ghosts" can do things like setting people on fire. They can attack in many ways because they are "zombies."

In the movie, the ghosts came into a house as fog and walked upside down on the ceiling, leaving behind wet footprints of the shoes or boots they were wearing. But it is not possible for ghosts to do so. Therefore, I can only imagine that someone with no real knowledge of ghosts made this movie.

Other horror movies are similar in this regard. One exorcism-related movie portrays a character doing a bridge like a gymnast and crawling down the stairs in the shape of a shrimp or turning her head around 360 degrees. For a real human, turning one's head around 360 degrees would break the neck, so this is impossible. It is also impossible to walk upside down. Such scenes are used as a way to frighten the audience, but I think they are so unrealistic that they make the movie less credible. Perhaps that is the only way moviemakers know how to portray fear.

Knowledge about the spiritual world will erase fear

As for myself, without realizing it, I have been talking with the spirits that have already left this world almost every day. When I first started communicating with spirits, I may have had some scary experiences, but after continuing to interact with spirits for nearly 40 years as part of my job, I do not particularly have any feelings of fear. This may be because of my spiritual power as well.

When I summon devils, evil spirits, or malicious spirits to conduct spiritual interviews at Happy Science, they seem quite tame, so it may cause some misunderstanding among the audience. When a malicious spirit possesses an average spiritual medium who might appear on TV to perform exorcisms, the medium often thrashes around in severe pain while sweating. In this sense, these spirits are indeed frightening. But whenever we conduct spiritual interviews at Happy Science, the spirits come at my request and leave when I ask them to. Most spirits obey my words, which may be why they do not seem so scary. There is such a difference because of the disparity in our spiritual powers.

Even when high spirits come down for a spiritual interview, it may look as if we are having a natural conversation, but this was not the case when I first began to channel spirits. I was in awe of the high spirits, who I thought were coming from a world far above us, and paid my respects as a human being. But as my level of enlightenment gradually rose and surpassed theirs, I clearly felt our positions reversing, so perhaps this is merely a relative matter.

Those who are completely ignorant of the spiritual world may find any spiritual matter scary or mysterious or may see it as something that makes them jump in fear. But there is nothing to be afraid of for those who understand the spiritual world well. Ordinary people may jump in fear if they see ghosts in the middle of the day, but spiritually well-versed people would only react mildly and simply tell them to go away because they are busy. Therefore, the situation would not escalate so far as to turn into a "sea of blood," as commonly depicted in horror movies. There is a significant difference between someone who knows about the spiritual world and those who do not. People fear spiritual beings because they have a foothold in this world and see things from a worldly perspective. They probably believe that the world beyond this one is a very scary place.

Without special conditions, spirits cannot exert direct influence in this world

Now, imagine that the afterworld is the true world and that we are spiritual beings living in a physical body. If we have this awareness, how would the world and our ways of life appear?

In this world, we have a physical body, which we govern and control. Our soul is inside this physical body, and the soul and body are connected by a silver cord and are unified as one. So it is normally impossible for other spirits to enter and take over our body. Spirits are just spiritual entities that do not possess physical bodies; so, in this world, we who have unified spiritual and physical bodies are essentially stronger than the spirits. Without a physical body, spirits cannot exert direct influence in this world unless special conditions are met.

In Western horror movies, ghosts are often portrayed to possess psychokinetic or psychic abilities to make physical phenomena happen. People in the West consume a lot of meat in their diet and use guns to kill others; in the old days, they would eat wild animals by hunting them with hatchets. So the spirits in the West may have strong psychokinetic powers, unlike the spirits in Japan. But, in general, spirits cannot move the physical objects of this world only with their spiritual bodies unless specific conditions are met. There are fewer than one in 10 spirits—or probably one in 100—that can move physical objects.

Moreover, even if a spirit were to cause a physical phenomenon, it tends to be perceived as a natural occurrence. For instance, if a draft came in, people might only think they left some windows open. Or if a book fell over, they might think it was due to an earthquake. So it is quite difficult for people to understand spiritual phenomena.

But I am sure you have occasionally experienced getting goose bumps as a child when you listened to or read scary stories or watched frightening movies or TV programs. Apparently, in Japan, the expression "getting goose bumps" is now often used in a positive way to describe something amazing or exciting. There was also a time in the past when it was used in this way, but it later gained a negative connotation and has been used to describe something scary for a long time, such as "getting goose bumps from sensing a spiritual presence." In recent times, however, an increasing number of people do not understand the meaning of the phrase, and the use of the phrase has switched back to describing happy events, such as "I got goose bumps when he gave me the diamond ring." The meaning of the expression has thus become unclear now.

Nevertheless, people do get goose bumps when talking about scary stories. I once talked to a foreigner about Nostradamus in English, and the person said, "I am getting goose bumps!" It was interesting to see how people of different races also experienced the same phenomenon. We sometimes experience phenomena that make our hair stand on end, and everyone has probably experienced a shiver running down their spine. Everyone has such kind of spiritual senses, but most people do not deeply explore them.

The reason why religious practitioners seclude themselves in the mountains

In general, society is full of vibrations called "beta waves," which interfere with our connection with the spirit world. These include TV, radio, music, conversations, and other noises. When there are various sounds, the connection with the spirit world becomes disconnected, as if a telephone line has been disrupted. Since the old days, many religious practitioners have secluded themselves in the mountains to undergo spiritual discipline alone, and the main reason for this is to avoid such interferences.

Nevertheless, they face many difficulties under such circumstances. For example, it is often said that during the Thousand-Day Circumambulation, when practitioners walk and meditate in the mountains, they face the devil's temptations while fasting in seclusion. This is because they have become extremely sensitive. They have also developed an acute sense of hearing, allowing them to hear the sounds and voices that normally cannot be heard.

Accumulating spiritual experiences by secluding oneself and shutting out worldly distractions has been a traditional method of spiritual training. People who do not have many such experiences cannot usually sense spiritual matters unless some physical phenomena happen to them. They may sense something if misfortunes, such as being involved in traffic accidents or fires, repeatedly befall them. Some phenomena occur to make people aware of the existence of the other world, but the number of reported cases has been decreasing.

2

The Truth about Will-O'-the-Wisps

Witnesses of will-o'-the-wisps during my childhood

During my childhood, many of my peers at the elementary school had seen will-o'-the-wisps, also known as *ignis fatuus*. A certain percentage of students had seen them, and the exact locations of the sightings could be determined.

An example of such a place is the schoolyard; it was located in the middle of a rice field on low ground behind Kawashima Elementary School, which I used to attend, but has now been rebuilt and turned into a nursery school. We would call it the "playground in the back"; it was a simple schoolyard with just a backstop. We often played what we called "baseball" using a softball. And, as the evening approached, we occasionally experienced something that scared us; it was a will-o'-the-wisp flying around the upper half of the backstop. Whenever someone noticed it and said, "Isn't that a will-o'-the-wisp?" the others responded, "Yes, you are right. Let's go home now." Such conversations were not uncommon in the countryside. We then quickly gathered our bats, balls, and gloves and rushed back home.

Another place where will-o'-the-wisps were frequently witnessed was near the Awa-Kawashima train station, which has appeared in some of the Happy Science movies. About 100–200 meters (110–220 yards) away from the train station in the direction of Tokushima station, there is a railway cutting through a hill, and on the right side of the hill is a graveyard. During the day, we as children would play hide-and-seek and explore the area by digging holes, much like in *The Adventures of Tom Sawyer*, and we were occasionally scolded by the landowner. But most children would go home once the sun set because there were many people who spoke of witnessing will-o'-the-wisps around there at dusk.

I also had the following experience, which I have already mentioned in various books. When I was in elementary school, I had a friend who was a year older than me. His house was not too far from mine; it was just beyond the nearby railway girder. I think his family was involved in farming. I often played *shogi* (Japanese chess) with him on a bench outside his house during my early years of elementary school.

About a week before his grandfather passed away, some neighbors witnessed a will-o'-the-wisp going in and out of my friend's two-story house through the roof. I heard this from several people and was amazed to hear about such an experience. Then, about a week later, my friend's grandfather actually passed away. I now understand that the souls of those whose deaths are near practice an "out-of-body experience" by occasionally leaving their physical bodies before they die. I think the soul of my friend's grandfather was going through such an experience. I have heard many similar stories.

When I was in elementary school, people commonly said that the will-o'-the-wisps that appear around the graveyard were phosphorus burning. But naturally, this does not seem right because it is questionable if any phosphorus is left in the body after it has been cremated. Phosphorus, which is used in match heads, is also inherent in human bodies, so some magazines for young boys made a plausible argument that burning phosphorus is the true nature of will-o'-the-wisps. Thinking about it, it should not be possible for phosphorus to suddenly catch fire and fly out of well-built graves that are not old and decaying. In any case, I often heard about the witnessing of will-o'-the-wisps.

Mysterious traits of will-o'-the-wisps

The latest instance I heard about will-o'-the-wisps was around the time of my father's death. My father (Honorary Adviser Saburo Yoshikawa) died on August 12, 2003, after being hospitalized and bedridden since May of that year. There was always someone visiting him in the hospital during the day, but my mother had not seen him for about three months because the hospital was a little far from her house.

Around the time my father died, many people, including the secretary attending to my mother, witnessed will-o'-the-wisps. For security reasons, a surveillance camera had been installed at the entrance of her house and it was facing the front gate.

According to my mother, it showed the footage of a number of will-o'-the-wisps flying around, and she got the shivers when she saw them. Because there were many of them, she assumed that other spirits had come from the other world to guide my father's soul, given that it was Obon season, a time when spirits in the other world are believed to come and visit their descendants.

In this way, will-o'-the-wisps can be recorded on camera, so there should be some scientific research to determine the nature of will-o'-the-wisps. A physicist at the Faculty of Science and Engineering at Waseda University, who does not believe in the existence of the other world, claims will-o'-the-wisps to be a plasma phenomenon. He created lab equipment to produce plasma and explained that the plasma was the true nature of the will-o'-the-wisp. But if this were true, there should not be any will-o'-the-wisps flying around because such equipment does not exist anywhere else. It is not possible to mistake them for fireflies either because their sizes are quite different.

I heard another story from my relatives in Kawashima Town during my elementary school days. During summer nights, they would go catch *ayu* (sweetfish) and eel by riding a wooden boat out toward a low-water bridge, which also appears in our movies. They would light up the riverbed with a lantern and harpoon the fish.

Ayu cannot be caught with bait because they only eat moss, so the only way to catch them was to use a decoy or a line that has many hooks. The movement of the fish becomes sluggish during the night, so it is easier to catch them by harpooning them from above. I believe my relatives were catching fish as their job.

One night, they saw a large will-o'-the-wisp flying down from above the low-water bridge. They said that it was so bright that they could even see the pebbles at the bottom of the riverbed. From this, I understood that will-o'-the-wisps possess a certain level of luminosity, which is quite mysterious.

Indispensable knowledge that helps you depart to the afterworld

Based on what I heard from the spirits that were identified as will-o'-the-wisps, they actually do not recognize themselves as such but feel as if they are flying in human form. We have discovered this as well.

As I have mentioned in *The Mystical Laws* (Tokyo: HS Press, 2015), another question about will-o'-the-wisps is, "What will happen if you put your hand through a will-o'-the-wisp?" Finding an answer to this question is quite a challenge that would be worth listing in the Guinness World Records. The timing to do this is extremely rare; nevertheless, two cases have been reported. According to these reports, will-o'-the-wisps are not so hot as to burn one's hands; one of them said it felt like cotton candy, whereas the other described it as the texture of silk. I understand what it feels like.

Will-o'-the-wisps themselves believe they still retain human form. This is a relative view, so from the point of view of the will-o'-the-wisps, people coming after them from below look like ogres trying to catch them when they are flying low in the sky. This is such a mysterious world. Various things can happen like this, so we need to know that after death, we can fly around as souls.

If we do not have the knowledge that human beings are essentially spiritual bodies, the departure to the afterlife will be rather difficult. To make the departure easier, some people have out-of-body experiences some time before death while their silver cords are still connected to their bodies. Some look at themselves lying in the hospital bed from above, whereas others meet their deceased relatives and ancestors. They often share such experiences with the people visiting them in the hospital, but such stories may not be taken seriously nowadays. In any case, it is important to know that spiritual bodies are the real entities of human beings.

Differences of ghost experiences between the West and the East

As I mentioned earlier, ghosts are more often depicted as zombies in the West and are considered to be resurrected from death. This may be due to the Egyptian tradition of mummification and the description of Jesus being resurrected in a physical body in the Bible. Descriptions of will-o'-the-wisps in Western works are rather uncommon.

In the East, on the contrary, will-o'-the-wisps are more common. They certainly appear in Chinese works, and they appear in Indian books as well. Many Indian books describe a small ball-like figure—slightly smaller than what we might generally imagine—emerging from around the chest. I believe many people in the East actually saw such things probably because many people practice meditation and yoga.

There are various cases in which spirits influence those who are living in this world. One such example is when spirits of those who recently passed away come to see the bereaved. Spirits also come to religions such as Happy Science or to those with a mission and teach about various things when necessary. In other cases, it is common for spirits that are unable to return to heaven to appear before the living people in places they had a connection to or through the relationships they had. These are also examples of ghost experiences.

3

Various Spiritual Experiences and Spiritual Fields

Questionable depictions in modern horror movies

Recent movies depict ghosts using cell phones, smartphones, and other electronic devices, so I can hardly keep up with such stories. In the movie *The Ring*, for example, when the characters insert a videotape into the videocassette player and watch it, they receive a phone call and die a week later. Receiving a phone call from a ghost is a strange idea; however, in addition to that, if the viewer shows the videotape to someone else, the curse is transferred to that person, like a chain letter of misfortune. Now that videotapes are no longer used, they seem to have been replaced by smartphones and other devices.

Although it is true that spirits have electrical properties in a sense, all the other depictions in the movie are unrealistic. The movie characters receive a phone call from the ghost, but where is the ghost calling from in the first place? Does it use a cell phone or a pay phone? This remains unclear, and I am also curious to know whether the ghost memorizes the phone numbers of the people it calls. I wonder whether the caller ID is even displayed on the cell phone screens.

This kind of plot may make the story more interesting, but I sometimes wonder if there are tech gadgets in the spirit world as well. I myself have not yet seen any areas in the spirit world with such tech gadgets, although I cannot deny their existence completely because it is possible for stray spirits wandering in computer-related companies to have some kind of electronic devices with them (in spiritual forms). If the souls of the people who worked on computers for decades become stray spirits after death, they may still have computers with them, so it cannot be denied altogether. But, in general, such electronic devices and other things of this world will no longer be available, and the spirits often cannot understand these devices.

In this sense, ghosts that can stay on a moving train are exceptional. Because trains go many miles an hour, the ghosts sitting on a train will usually be left behind on the train tracks when the train moves. So the ghosts that can stay on board should be flying at a high speed. Sitting on a moving train is a very difficult thing to do; the ghosts must have an awareness that enables them to remain on board without being thrown out.

My experience of escaping sleep paralysis

Some of you may have experienced the spirit world or have had ghost experiences in one way or another. I, too, have had many such experiences, as I have written in other books.

My family owned a secondary house, as depicted in some of the Happy Science movies. It was once a factory that my father ran as a young man, but it was deserted after he closed his business. The first floor was left unused and gave off a scary atmosphere, but I used the second floor as my study room; I would go there to study in the evenings. It was indeed a scary place. It was pitch-dark, so I had to carry a flashlight to go in and turn on the light in the room. As a child, it felt like I was going to a haunted house to test my courage every night.

One afternoon, perhaps on a holiday, I was taking a nap there when I felt something pressing down on my chest, and I experienced something similar to sleep paralysis. I could clearly see two dark hands pushing down on my chest; I could also see a dark shadow—probably a face—but could not see the lower part of its body. Because it was pushing down on me, I was unable to move no matter how hard I tried. In the end, I managed to rotate my body to the right side and roll off the *futon* (Japanese mattress) to escape it. This was how I learned to escape sleep paralysis, although I have not had any similar experiences since then.

In general, under sleep paralysis, you have difficulty breathing and cannot move your body. So if you ever experience this and cannot move, I recommend you try rotating your body to the side and rolling off the bed. You might fall onto the floor, but this is an effective way to free yourself from sleep paralysis. It seems like ghosts are not good at stopping side turns. Although you cannot raise your body to sit up, you can move sideways because they do not seem to know how to stop it.

My experience of exploring the spirit world that extends under the ground

Another experience I clearly remember is one I had around fifth grade. At Kawashima Shrine in my hometown, there was a fall festival. Because most townspeople were shrine parishioners, the elementary school students would wear *happi* jackets and *hachimaki* headbands, carry the *mikoshi* (portable shrine), and walk around the town. Much like during Halloween, we would walk around collecting offerings instead of candy.

After the festival that day, I had a high fever because I was really exhausted and also perhaps because it was a hot day. Thinking back on it now, it was probably due to some spiritual influence because I carried the *mikoshi*. But I did not understand that at the time. I had a fever without any specific causes and my body temperature rose to nearly 40°C (104°F). I remember sleeping on a water pillow with an ice bag hanging from the ceiling to cool my head.

Then, I got the feeling of being sucked into the ground. I was pulled down through a tunnel-like hole until I was at the center of the Earth. As I was descending, I saw various worlds depending on the depth. When I reached the center of the Earth, however, I could not return by the way I came. I saw magma there so I tried hard to go back, but I just could not. Then, I thought I could perhaps get through to the other side of the Earth, and as soon as I tried to move in that direction, I suddenly found myself popping out from the other side of the Earth. That was how I made it back home.

This happened 52 or 53 years ago, but I still remember it. The vision was so clear, distinct, and colorful that it has lingered in my memory; it was too vivid to call it a dream. It was most probably an experience of the spirit world or an exploration of it.

I think the spirit world—mostly the realm of hell—extends under the surface of the Earth. I saw everything all the way down to where there was magma; that place is probably the true nature of what is called Burning Hell or Scorching Hell. I assume a certain type of spirit world exists around the magma layer, where souls are tormented by the heat. These souls are mostly the ones who are seized by uncontrollable rage. I once visited such a place.

Places with strong spiritual magnetic fields

We can find similar spiritual fields, which cannot be seen with the physical eye, in various places on Earth as well. There are locations in Japan that are sometimes called "power spots" (places where you can get spiritual energy) and these places attract young female visitors. This term is usually used rather lightly, but there are certain places with very strong spiritual magnetic fields; there is no doubt that these places are true "power spots." There are special spiritual fields in such places, and the spirit world exists in many of them.

For example, there are spiritual fields in mountains that attract people's faith or places where ascetics have been training themselves since the old days, and these spiritual fields exist in the spirit world as well. A place such as Mt. Fuji, which attracts people's faith, is one example. Such spiritual fields exist in large numbers inside and at the foot of Mt. Fuji. Mt. Aso also has such fields, and there are spiritual fields in Tokushima Prefecture as well. Thus, a spiritual field is often found in places that attract strong faith or that have large spiritual ruins. In many cases, these power spots are connected to other places as well.

Shambhala, which has an access point around Tibet, is an especially well-known place. It is generally believed that there is a spiritual field in the Himalayas called Shambhala, where yogis and *sennin* (hermits) undergo ascetic training. This is often talked about within the circles of theosophy. I think some people undergoing spiritual training in India and some *sennin*-type people in China have actually visited this place.

Indeed, there is a spiritual magnetic field for spiritual training inside the tallest mountains on Earth. Some souls go there to undergo spiritual training after death, and there are also cases where yogis and *sennin* send their souls there to undergo spiritual training while they are still alive.

Spirits carry out various kinds of training, and most of them seek to attain a higher level of spiritual awakening. Among them, there are a certain number of spiritual leaders referred to as "masters." There are also those who are called "avatars" instead of "masters"; they are usually a little superior to masters. Avatars are great spiritual masters who normally give guidance on special, secret training in the spirit world, but they are also born on earth once every few thousand years to be a savior or to launch a great spiritual revolution. Some spirits from these high-level classes also train themselves or guide others at such places.

Such training places do exist, though there are of course spirits that do not go there and reside in the higher realms of heaven in the spirit world. As far as I have seen, there are at least several thousand spirits undergoing spiritual training at this kind of training center in the spirit world.

4

The Realms of *Tengu, Sennin, Yokai,* and *Youko*

Some spirits stray from the path as they strive to acquire force

Many spirits train themselves to gain spiritual awakening and acquire the so-called force, but there are spirits that gradually stray from the path. As they seek to achieve self-realization through spiritual powers, they end up going off the main road. They become too focused on spiritual influences, mystical powers, and miracles and neglect to explore the right way of life as a human or the right way of spiritual life in the afterworld. Whereas the royal road of angels and bodhisattvas must be to guide people on earth in the right direction, they take more interest in their own special abilities.

This tendency is observed in the characters of the American movie *Doctor Strange*, for example. The characters create rings of light to fight; in the same way, there are spirits that use force. But whether such forces have the same power as true spiritual enlightenment is somewhat questionable. Many angels, archangels, bodhisattvas, and tathagatas also possess mystical powers, but those on the royal road try to guide people through teachings, unlike those that focus on using these powers.

So there are spirits that grant people mystical powers in a visible way. These spirits, who undergo spiritual training but do not take the royal road of angels and bodhisattvas, have formed their own worlds, apart from what is known as heaven and hell. These are the *Tengu* (long-nosed goblin) Realm, *Sennin* Realm, and the realm inhabited by *yokai* (monsters and goblins). These spirits are not exactly demons or devils. But they are mostly interested in gaining recognition and respect from the world by boosting their spiritual powers through egocentric efforts and achieving self-realization. Many of them also strive to get rid of their enemies using their supernatural powers.

Tengu *have strong willpower to achieve rapid growth but often fall from power*

In Japan, there are many *tengu* that use force-type spiritual power probably because of the traditional practice of ascetic training in the mountains. They sometimes do good work, but they are not always good because they have strong, selfish desires to benefit themselves.

Tengu are known for their mischievous tendencies and experiences of downfall. Because they have very strong willpower, when they are born on earth, they can rapidly develop their business or climb the ladder of success as politicians in a short period of time, but they will eventually fall from power.

Tengu could be found among samurai as well. For example, there were many *tengu* in the Heike clan in 12th-century Japan. Taira no Kiyomori (1118–1181) rapidly rose to power and became the ruler in a single lifetime; it was said that only people from the Heike clan counted as human. But Kiyomori's rapid downfall and the ruin of his clan that followed illustrate a typical pattern of *tengu*. Although *tengu* achieve rapid growth, they fail in the end because they essentially do not have sincere love at heart.

Yokai *take pleasure in frightening or scaring people*

The world of *yokai* is often portrayed in Japanese anime and manga. Because the spirit world is the "world of creation"—a world where anything can be created—different life forms can be created using life energy. For this reason, anything that can be imagined by humans can exist there; many ancient living things that do not exist in this world or those that have gone extinct can also be found in the spirit world.

Among these creatures are *yokai*, which take pleasure in frightening or scaring people. Their awareness is not high enough to be able to teach Buddha's Truth, but because they can use mysterious powers, some of them train themselves to have a better command of those powers. They often practice shape-shifting, and after continuously practicing it, they may have become what they are because of their lives in the distant past.

In Japan, *yokai* are mostly raccoon dogs and foxes, but foxes greatly outnumber raccoon dogs and represent *yokai* in general. There are also many other types of *yokai*. These *yokai* have "transformable bodies" and are able to morph into something different.

Even among those who were born as humans with human spirits, there may be some who resemble certain animals. This has commonly been explained as relating to soul siblings, but in the context of Japanese Shinto, some actually have a "transformable body" and can turn into an animal. For example, some can morph into tigers whereas others morph into large snakes, dragons, or enormous birds; they often have such "transformable bodies." If one has gained this ability of self-transformation, it is possible to shape-shift in the spirit world.

Some of them use this ability to frighten those that live in the ordinary spirit world, and they take pleasure in doing so. Although they retain such childish tendencies, they often demonstrate amazing skills of craftsmanship. There are such types of people among those who work with the mentality of an artisan.

Sennin *have special abilities but tend to lack interpersonal skills*

There are also spirits called *sennin*. They do not behave as nonsensically as *yokai* do, and they are a little different from *tengu*. Many of them used to be religious practitioners, such as ascetic monks, but have strayed from the right path after going through extensive physical ascetic training.

Everyone actually has *sennin*-like powers; all religious practitioners in India are said to be *sennin*, so the term does not always carry a negative connotation. If the spirits lack spiritual training to take the royal road, they tend to develop unsociable characteristics. When they are born into this world, they often become the type of people who display some kind of special abilities, or an exceptional ability as engineers or specialists, but lack interpersonal skills.

Tengu, sennin, *and* yokai *are unleashed for bringing innovation to the world*

Thus, there are realms of *tengu*, *yokai*, and *sennin*, but it is hard to know whether the outward appearances of these spirits reflect their true figures. Because they can cause many changes to occur, it is difficult to know what is truly going on; they sometimes commit mischief in this world, cause confusion in the heavenly world, or go to the world of hell to make various things happen.

Once in a while, the world needs change. When it is time to make a drastic change in an era, the doors to the realms of *tengu*, *sennin*, and *yokai* will open, allowing these spirits to be born on earth. Not all of them can be born, but it is easier for them to be born on earth in times of confusion.

One such example was during the period of warring states when the tide of the era greatly changed. Various factors are necessary for the times to change, so these spirits are often released for the purposes of bringing innovation to the world.

Among the warlords during the period of warring states, there were angels as well as *tengu*-type people. There were also those who were attuned to the devils in hell while they were alive and went to hell after death. In reality, people who have come from different realms are competing for power on earth.

Differences in character between tengu, sennin, *and* yokai

There is a Japanese historical TV drama series called *Kirin ga Kuru* ("Awaiting Kirin") that aired in 2020. The main character and samurai, Mitsuhide Akechi (1528–1582), seemed to have had some degree of faith, but the first lord he served, Dosan

Saito (1494–1556), who fought to conquer and rule present-day Gifu Prefecture, was a typical *tengu*. There are certainly people like him. In modern times, many *tengu* can be found among politicians as well as in rapidly growing companies.

Interestingly, in contrast, there are many *sennin* in technology companies that require technical skills or in the rapidly advancing fields of high technology. In fact, they are trying to bring various skills that are available in the spirit world to this world using worldly materials. I think they are researching into such matters. Inventors who seem a little eccentric or odd are often *sennin*. Some of them do good work, but they are hardly ever recognized and create discord.

Nevertheless, a certain number of these spirits are needed in this world. Those who are eager to expand their power or desperately seek to attain a higher status are often *tengu*-type people, whereas those who become intoxicated with advanced skills are mostly *sennin*-type people. *Yokai*-type people are often two-faced because they dislike their true nature being exposed. I have an impression that there is a disparity between their outward attitudes and their true intentions or the actions they take in secret. These three types of beings have the ability to travel between heaven, the spirit world overlapping with the earthly world, and hell. These are the important points to remember.

Fox-type and snake-type spirits have an influence in nightlife districts

In terms of spiritual entities, the number of fox-type spirits is especially high in Japan. Because there are many *Inari* shrines (that worship fox deities) around the country, these spirits attract faith from many people, which gives them a certain level of spiritual power. When people strongly desire worldly benefits, they earnestly pray at such shrines, so the fox-type spirits have gained a certain level of spiritual power.

Inari worship can be seen in many places in Japan, so there are many fox-type spirits and *youko*-type spirits (bewitching fox spirits) that appear under various names of gods. I think many mediums, fortune-tellers, and founders of small religious groups in local areas are of this type. These spirits can make small miracles happen, but I am not sure if they are good influences in the long run.

In addition to fox-type spirits, there are snake-type spirits. Snake-type spirits are often connected to sexual matters, so if you are too involved with such spirits, you will most likely be led or dragged down to the Hell of Beasts or the Hell of Lust. If you are tricked by them, you will most likely meet such an end, so it is better not to go along with them for too long.

Many people who work in the nightlife business visit *Inari* shrines to pray for the prosperity of their business; the spirits they pray to actually bring customers to their shops and bars. There are many nightlife districts even now, and these spirits come to the entrances of such areas and work to lure customers to the storefront. In addition to barkers, spiritual entities tout prospective customers.

Businesspeople who often visit such places are probably affected by these spirits, but usually, the spirits will not linger around them for more than an overnight stay. These businesspeople will bring one spirit home after enjoying drinking, but once they go to work the next day, the possessing spirit will move away from them to possess another person. Then, the person who becomes possessed next will be drawn to nightlife. Their connection is mostly this shallow, but if you go to such places too often, the spirits may stay longer and settle down.

Nevertheless, there is a positive side to this. If you have this type of spirit with you, you will become more susceptible to inspiration, be able to make accurate guesses on various things, or be able to detect things. So, not everything about it is negative.

I heard that some business executives take their subordinates to the bars in the Ginza or Shimbashi area in Tokyo to ask the hostesses to guess which person is likely to be promoted to a higher position. They apparently do such "inspections" on their personnel, which surprisingly often turn out to be accurate.

Spiritual traits of fortune-tellers

There are many fortune-tellers, including palm readers and diviners who use the eight trigrams. When I was young, I checked out a few palm readers and fortune-tellers who practiced onomancy after I gained spiritual powers. Based on what I saw, they are actually receiving some inspiration from the spiritual beings that are with them. But after I had my fortune told, I felt as if I had come in contact with an amphibian or a frog with slimy skin. In most cases, I had the feeling of touching something gloomy and sticky; many of the fortune-tellers were the type of people we would not encounter in any other field.

Those who are engaged in Western fortune-telling may receive guidance from witches. I do not have enough experience to say anything definite, but it is possible that witches are with them.

Although there are mere imposters who pretend to be fortune-tellers, there are usually some spiritual beings that give inspiration to those who do fortune-telling for work. But I am not sure of what these beings truly are. Although fortune-tellers may believe that they are receiving guidance from *sennin*-type spirits, based on the slimy and sticky feeling I perceived, I would guess that these spirits are something closer to amphibians or the types of beings between *sennin* and *yokai*. They are most likely connected to such beings that secretly inhabit remote worlds.

5

Spiritual Training Needed
When You Become Spiritually Sensitive

Makeup tests to become angels

I talked about a variety of subjects. Ultimately, we all live as humans while our souls inhabit a human body, and our souls also take the human form. We live in this world for a number of decades as an individual human being, and when we return to the other world after death, we continue to live there under the same name, appearance, and gender we had on earth until we are reborn next. This is the most common case. But the souls that have accumulated special experiences over a long time will often regain their original forms shortly after they return to the other world.

In the case of those aiming to be angels, souls need to take a series of tests of different levels even in the other world and undergo initiation to advance to a higher level. If they lack the experience of helping others during their time on earth, they continue to help and guide the people on earth after returning to the other world. They need to cultivate virtue by assisting the people of this world as guiding spirits or supporting spirits; otherwise, they cannot get a chance to ascend to a higher level.

So these spirits give spiritual guidance to the people who are contributing to the world, cure illnesses of those who still have a mission to fulfill, or save them from an imminent accident. There are many spirits that do these things as tests to make up for the lack of their spiritual training in the process of becoming angels or bodhisattvas.

Of course, there are also real angels or bodhisattvas who come to help and protect those who have very important missions to fulfill on earth.

Human beings can create illnesses and also make them disappear

Human beings can create illnesses. Humans are life energy itself, so we can alter part of this life energy to create even an ailment. Whereas it is possible to make an illness disappear, it is also possible to create an illness.

For example, if you are on the receiving end of someone's strong grudge or, in other words, if you are possessed by someone's *ikiryo* (spirit of a living person) and are constantly under that person's curse, an evil spirit that is attuned to that *ikiryo* can come and lend power to it. Then, a lesion can develop in your body. It does not take long for this to happen; a lesion can develop in less than a day. However, by having the right faith and becoming connected to a righteous guiding spirit, you can make the lesion disappear.

Since 2020, there has been a lot of news about the coronavirus that originated in China. Looking at the spherical, microscopic coronavirus, I understand that a new disease was intentionally created. It has been created based on certain intentions, but because there are various kinds of divine will behind the disease, I cannot make a sweeping statement about it.

The importance of being humble, sincere, honest, and diligent

Even if you become spiritually sensitive, you need to be wary because you can head into different directions depending on who is spiritually guiding you. I am a powerful spiritual magnet myself, so many of those who read my books, listen to my lectures, are in close contact with me, or are near me are affected and often find that they have also become "magnetized." When this happens, they may become more susceptible to inspiration or may gain the ability to spiritually sense things or read other people's minds. In many cases, they become partly able to channel spirits, so they need to be particularly careful of the following things.

If they give themselves too much credit or are too preoccupied by how great they were in their past lives, unguarded areas will be created in their minds. Then, they will most likely allow evil beings to enter their minds, contrary to people's expectations of them becoming angels after having gained the ability to channel spirits to a certain extent. It is very difficult to stop this from happening.

When one becomes able to channel spirits to a greater extent, it is like the windows of a house being left open. Even if the front door is locked, it is still possible to enter the house because the windows are open. Unless you learn to open and close these windows at will, spirits will be able to freely enter. Among the spirits that wander around in this world, there are many evil beings. Some people are possessed by these beings, and there are also others who send out many evil thoughts. So when you notice that the "window of your mind" is beginning to open and you start to experience some spiritual phenomena, it is important to follow the righteous spiritual training. It is extremely important to be sincere, to make diligent efforts, to be humble, and to be honest.

If you have characteristics that resemble animals, such as foxes, raccoon dogs, snakes, or other animals, I recommend that you strive to eliminate those qualities. Check and see if you do not have anger or hatred toward others, desires to exclude, deceive, or cheat others, or thoughts of defrauding others of their money. Also, check for any desires to give yourself too much credit and flatter yourself or wishes for others to fail or fall from grace. If you harbor such negative thoughts after having gained spiritual abilities, you will be approached by beings that respond to those thoughts and may end up facing your own destruction, or bad incidents may happen to the people you have negative thoughts toward. Therefore, as your spiritual awareness advances or your spiritual senses sharpen, you need to be more humble, sincere, honest, and diligent and make efforts to be a decent human being.

Judging right and wrong based on morals and common sense

As I said in the beginning, if people delve too deeply into academic studies of this world, they tend to become less susceptible to inspiration and start to disbelieve spiritual matters. As a result, there will be an increasing number of people who believe in atheism and materialism. So there is a dangerous side to academic studies. On the contrary, among the founders of long-standing new religions, there were many who did not study very much. Many of them did not understand what is good and evil and could not distinguish between things they should and should not do in this world.

Even if you are pure-hearted and spiritually sensitive in the beginning, when you stand in a position of managing an organization and have influence over many people, you must make an effort to study what you should and should not do based on the laws and morals of this world. You need to be able to understand, discern, and judge these things.

So look at yourself as if looking into a mirror and see if anything is crooked or odd. Judge yourself through the fruits of your actions as well, and see if your deeds have not deluded or misled people or made them unhappy. It is important to reflect on these things.

Once you become susceptible to inspiration, you may think that you can write any number of novels, for example. But if you constantly write murder mysteries, you will end up in a bad place after death. Many souls of criminals who were executed in prison would come to give you inspiration and tell you how they had killed someone. You may be amazed by the new ways to kill a person and find it amusing to write about it, but even if your novels were to sell well, there will be nothing good waiting for you later on. You will end up in a bad place.

Therefore, instead of taking pride in your ability to read other people's minds or perceive various things, you need to remind yourself that your mind is also like glass that can be seen through. So you need to strive further to make your mind much clearer.

Although too much worldly knowledge will weigh you down and make you insensitive, like wearing a suit of armor, you need to be aware of the appropriate moral code and common sense that enable you to judge what is right and wrong. On the other hand, people who are well-versed in worldly matters, have abundant worldly knowledge, and are competent at work need to cultivate a transparent heart—a heart that understands poetry. It is important to have a pure heart to be able to savor poetry.

If you frequently go out for drinks to chat with people, enjoy gambling such as horse racing, *keirin* (bicycle racing), mahjong, and pachinko, get involved with delinquents or criminals, or visit spiritually impure places, you will become attuned to such negative spiritual influences. So it is best to ward off such influences and stay away from them. There is very little benefit in approaching them. It is important to stay away from them as much as possible and correct your lifestyle. In terms of what you read, listen, and watch, it is also important to focus on positive things rather than on negative ones.

6

Ways to Deal with Malicious Spirits and Devils

Those possessed by malicious spirits cannot study my teachings

Those who are truly possessed by malicious spirits or low-level demons will show the following traits. There are different levels of devils, and even a low-level demon or low-level devil can destroy a family or company.

In general, those who are constantly possessed by such beings are unable to read my books. Even if you give my books on the basic Truth to those suspected to be possessed by evil spirits, they probably will not be able to read them. I have seen many such cases. When they try to read the book, they can see and read the letters, but the meaning of the words will not sink into their minds. The contents of the book are repelled, so they cannot understand them even if they read them.

The same is true for my lectures on tape, CDs, or DVDs; in less than five minutes of playing one, the possessing spirits will find it unbearable and flee. There are also cases when the person being possessed falls asleep.

I talked about this in the past: When I was working in a trading house, I had a coworker who was possessed by *inugami* (evil dog spirits). More than 20 evil dog spirits had possessed him; unfortunately, as a newly hired employee in a business suit and tie, I could not completely dispel them.

He was apparently considered to be an outstanding employee when he first started work, but he was eventually shunned by others and was treated as deadwood. Because he had some understanding of spiritual matters, he came to me for help. I had him listen to one of the recorded spiritual messages, and in less than five minutes, he fell asleep before my eyes. I had only heard of snot bubbles in stories, but at that time, I actually saw him sleeping and blowing a snot bubble right in front of me. This was because the possessing spirits prevented him from listening to the spiritual messages from the high spirits, so he could not listen to them at all. Evil spirits will prevent you from hearing my lectures, so please watch out for this.

Similar things can happen to people attending my lectures and viewing our movies. Of course, there are cases where the contents are too difficult to understand for someone with no knowledge of the Truth. Small children may not be able to understand them, either. I have to acknowledge that there are some exceptions, but in general, when people physically cannot hear or understand the contents of my lectures and our movies, including the CDs and DVDs, or feel as if something is covering their ears, then it is most certainly because they are constantly under spiritual possession.

If this is the case for you, you must make up your mind to

fight; otherwise, your destination after death is most likely determined. These spirits will most certainly take you to their realms after death, and even before you die, it is highly likely that many misfortunes will befall the people around you, including your family.

Fight with prayers and Kigan while knowing the limit of your abilities

There was a time when some Happy Science local branches actively welcomed people who were suffering from severe mental illnesses and performed exorcisms on them. But oftentimes, the possessing spirits were stronger than the branch managers, leading to the failure of the exorcisms. So I told them not to do too much of it.

The human body is like a house. Some houses are still habitable after repairs, but there are others that are beyond repair; these are houses with rotten pillars, broken windows, and holes in the walls. If someone is mentally damaged to the point where they resemble an abandoned house in the fields, the person is unfortunately under total control of the spirits possessing him or her. Although the person's spiritual body is still connected to the physical body by the silver cord, the spiritual body has already been kicked out, allowing other spirits to control the body, behave violently, and do anything they want.

There are uncontrollable people who act violently or inflict violence on their family members at home, but these people have adopted completely different personalities. In such cases, their souls have left the physical bodies and are wandering around, while different brutal spirits take over their bodies. Some people can still be saved, but at such a level, they tend to react very violently to any words of Truth. They may throw or break things, or they might even threaten to kill you with a knife. This is an unfortunate situation, but there must have been a reason for them to have accumulated so much negativity.

Once they exceed a certain level, there is not much others can do for them but pray. If you try to deal with them head-on, they may resist and act out violently. So the only option would either be to pray or seek help from someone who is more virtuous and at a higher spiritual level than you.

You can visit a Happy Science shoja (temple) and request a Kigan (ritual prayer), for example. Kigan is effective even when it is remotely performed; even if the possessed person is not aware of the Kigan taking place, it is still possible to remove the spirit possessing him or her. There are times when a remote Kigan is better because directly approaching the possessed person can make him or her act very violently. What is more, such a person usually cannot even step foot into the entrance of the Happy Science local branch or shoja.

There is a certain correlation between one's spiritual power and his or her power of exorcism, so it is important to know what you can and cannot do. You need to know the limits of your abilities and be aware that you need further spiritual training to do what is beyond your capacity now.

Keep your distance from odd religious groups and spiritual phenomena

I myself give spiritual messages, but there are times when I have the spirits enter and speak through other channelers. However, if these channelers lack spiritual training and the spirits are stronger than them, it is possible for these spirits to remain in the channelers' bodies. Sometimes evil spirits and devils cannot be removed, which is truly scary. So you should not rejoice too much that you can channel spirits or give spiritual messages. You must do so within the range of your abilities. There are times when the saying, "Far from Jupiter, far from his thunder," applies to such negative influences.

Sometimes your situation can get worse after visiting certain religious groups, shrines, and temples in search of salvation. There are misguided religious groups and mediums that are possessed by strong devils. When you visit those places, the low-level demons and evil spirits possessing you may flee in the presence of stronger devils, but it is better to keep your distance from such places that overall seem suspicious.

I have talked about various topics about the secret world of religion, including many introductory points. I hope they will be helpful to you in some way.

CHAPTER TWO

Recovering from Spiritual Disturbance

Secrets about the Viral Infection and
Spiritual Possession

Originally recorded in Japanese on March 28, 2020,
at the Special Lecture Hall of Happy Science in Japan,
and later translated into English.

1

Spiritual Truth behind Viral Infections and Illnesses

Indispensable knowledge that is not taught at school

This chapter deals with a basic topic—a theme that is unavoidable for those involved in religion. This is the kind of knowledge we must have as humans living on earth, but it is one of the truths that are not taught through education, academic studies, or science.

While living in our physical bodies, we are constantly affected by various spiritual beings, and we undergo many changes due to those influences. We ourselves are spiritual beings dwelling inside physical bodies, and we are also influenced by external factors. We live under the law of action and reaction in this way.

If we develop a certain tendency, we will start to live in a distorted way. Then, the spiritual beings that have the same tendency will gather around that distorted part. This is a simple truth, but unfortunately, many people do not understand it. Although this should be properly taught at home and at school from an early age, it is difficult to do so. Furthermore, not many people come to study this at a religion, which is quite regrettable.

Viral infections are a kind of spiritual possession

Using the expression "spiritual disturbance" may make my talk a little difficult to understand, so let me explain it in simple terms. To take a recent case as an example, the novel coronavirus is spreading all over the world, and hundreds of thousands of people were already infected by the time I gave this lecture in March 2020. I was certain that the number of infected people would soon surpass one million and reach several million with a death toll of over hundreds of thousands.

Even if people contract the coronavirus, there are those with average physical strength who get well and make a full recovery and others who become severely infected and die from developing pneumonia. The death rate varies from country to country, but it does not seem so different compared with the death rate resulting from the flu.

Based on my observations and experiences, it is clear that the flu is caused by spiritual possession. The flu mostly spreads during the cold months, and this coincides with the time when a large number of insects and bugs die due to the sudden drop in temperature. In fact, many of them become stray spirits, and these stray spirits stick around in groups, floating like soap bubbles near the surface of the earth, in the fields and trees, and even in the cities.

Among the people walking in the city, there are those who become possessed by these stray spirits and others who do not.

When a person is possessed by a group of spirits, the person will gradually become the host and "rent out" his or her body to these spirits to coexist. Then, the spirits will spread inside the person's body and gradually erode it. In the worst-case scenario, this could lead to the person's death. So even small spirits, which normally do not seem to have a will of their own, can cause illnesses when working together as a group.

Illnesses and bad physical conditions can be caused by spiritual influence

In the case of the flu, especially a virulent one, sometimes a human spirit can be found at the core of the spirit group consisting of the souls of viruses and bacteria. In general, there is only one human spirit in the case of the flu, but this spirit is not necessarily of someone who died from the flu—it can also be a lost spirit of someone who died in the hospital from some kind of illness or an unexpected cause. Such spirits have the same kind of desire as the souls of the dead viruses, bacteria, bugs, and insects; they all want to regain the life they once had by possessing people. They have this desire to be resurrected.

When you are possessed by these spirits, you will start to have a high fever or show symptoms that are exactly like the ones the deceased person showed just before his or her death. If you can overcome these symptoms, the spirits will leave your body after a week or so. This type of spiritual possession is more likely to occur when you have poor physical strength.

What I just stated most probably applies to coronavirus infections as well. It is said that more people will be infected in the coming months, but so far, the rate of infected cases in Japan is much lower than that of car accidents (at the time of the lecture). So, although viruses are everywhere, there are people who get infected and those who do not.

In fact, infections occur based on the same principle as spiritual possession. Therefore, once you meet the conditions to prevent spiritual possession from happening, you will be able to repel the viruses; no matter how hard they try to possess you, they will not be able to. This is the same as oil repelling water. So just because there are viruses and bacteria does not mean you will always become sick. Large numbers of various viruses and bacteria exist everywhere all year round, so please understand it as such.

In some cases, spiritual possession can cause diseases, and it can also lead to minor health problems. Even if you go to a hospital due to pain in a particular part of your body, doctors are often unable to medically determine the cause. There are many cases when doctors cannot identify the cause of an ailment, which is unfortunate. Doctors try hard to statistically examine the similarities among the patients who contract the same disease, but in many cases, they cannot identify the root cause. That is because many illnesses that arise for unknown reasons are actually caused by spiritual influences.

Souls that end up falling to the Hell of Beasts and turning into animals

In the spirit world, where we go in the afterlife, spirits of animals exist in addition to human spirits. Although people in modern society may find it hard to understand, there are also human spirits that have fallen to the Hell of Beasts and have turned into animals such as cows and horses, just like the parents of the main character from the novel *Toshishun* written by Ryunosuke Akutagawa.

Each animal has its own distinctive characteristics. When people live in such a way that they share similar qualities or tendencies as a specific animal, their souls will most likely fall to a place called the Hell of Beasts after death and take a similar form as that animal. If they stay in the animal form for too long, they could forget that they were originally human spirits and start to believe the animal form they see as their true self. This is very sad, but this happens because the mind can attune to 3,000 worlds and one's thoughts can manifest in 3,000 different ways, as taught in the later generations of Buddhism.

The notion of human souls turning into animal form is not only taught in Buddhism. In Plato's *The Republic*, there is a description of his teacher Socrates explaining how human souls can turn into animal figures. According to certain descriptions, some souls choose to turn into swans to show scrupulousness, whereas others choose to be different wild animals; when the souls go on to the other world, they take different forms depending on which openings they go through. So the transformation of souls into animal form is described in Western philosophy as well. I assume deep-sighted spiritual mediums can understand such spiritual truths.

Check and see if you have adopted any characteristics of animals

If human souls take on animal forms after death, it is because they share the same characteristics as the soul each animal symbolizes. For example, lions symbolize courage. Those who are more inclined to deceive, commit fraud, lie, or cheat will become like a fox. Those with a strong tendency to avoid people, run away, or hide will turn into a rat-like figure. The type that always stings anyone who comes close to them will turn into a porcupine-like figure.

Some people display characteristics of hyenas that flock to dead animals to feed on them. This is not a pleasant sight, but whenever someone or something dies, hyenas or vultures always gather from nowhere. When one hyena or vulture shows up, the others also follow and feed on the carcasses. In this way, there are animals that are highly responsive to the smell of something rotten.

There are also snake spirits that often possess people. There are many snakes living in nature, but apart from those, there are many human spirits in the Hell of Beasts that have turned into a snake-like figure. As you can see, snakes have qualities of being ferocious, being obsessive, and having strong sexual desires, grudges, or suspicions. Those who display strong tendencies like these are apt to become snakes after death.

When relationships become entangled in a love triangle, the person involved may begin to look like a snake, or the person may also attract a snake spirit. Of course, it can also be some other animal spirit. There are animals that symbolize greed and others that represent various qualities.

Therefore, when you practice self-reflection to see if you are under spiritual disturbance, I advise you to examine whether your personality resembles the characteristics of a specific animal. You could even go to a zoo or browse through an animal encyclopedia to do this. Whereas some animals are calm and peaceful, other animals have unpleasant characters. So please check and see if you have not adopted similar qualities as these animals.

In regard to the snake spirits I just mentioned, there are people who develop rheumatism from being possessed by snake spirits. When I spiritually see or shed God's Light on people with poor blood circulation, pain, or immobility in the legs, I sometimes discover snake spirits possessing them. There are also cases where fox spirits are possessing people. People may think they have stiff shoulders due to older age, but it could be fox spirits causing pain by possessing their shoulders or the back of their head.

Misfortunes can occur in the family due to the influence of animal spirits

Although animals are higher organisms than insects, many animals cannot comprehend the other world even after they die. Animals want to live in this world by feeding on something, but they could die from food shortages in the winter. In modern society, many animals are hit by cars and killed in accidents. Some are killed by people. In Japan, there was a year when 5,000 bears were shot and killed by hunters because an increasing number of bears were appearing in the villages in search of food.

From the animals' perspective, they cannot understand why they have to be killed because it is natural for them to look for food. That is why some of them are unable to return to heaven immediately after death. Even bears have families—mother bears, father bears, and young cubs. If they were shot and killed while just looking for food for their family, they could end up becoming lost spirits. Wild monkeys and wild boars can also come to the villages in search of food.

In some cases, even livestock domesticated for meat can form groups of lost spirits. For this reason, I think it is better for farms, slaughterhouses, or meat processing plants that handle domesticated animals and sell the meat to occasionally offer prayers to console the souls of those animals. People who kill many animals as part of their job need to be careful because misfortunes and tragedies often befall the family members of people with such jobs.

The same can be said of Shinto priests and Buddhist monks who perform exorcisms and ritual prayer at their shrines or temples. We often hear about their family members dying in mysterious ways, suffering physical disabilities, or contracting inexplicable illnesses. This is most probably because the priests and monks are not spiritually strong enough to handle the many rituals and prayers they perform and are too burdened by the thought energy they receive from people. As a result, their family members could be affected.

2

Spiritual Disturbance Caused by Excessive Burden

When your life, work, and personality start to collapse

Because spiritual influences cannot be seen with the eyes, people try to identify a materialistic cause for illnesses and misfortunes based on materialistic thinking. But there are many cases in which unseen influences are at work. Based on my experience as a company employee, more than 50 percent of the people today seem to be under some kind of spiritual possession.

For this reason, it would be spiritually difficult to be in packed trains during rush hours. The situation might be better in offices, where each employee has his or her own separate desk. But in Japanese companies, where workers must sit close to each other, the spirits possessing other people can come to bother you, so it can also be difficult. In this way, we are constantly affected by spiritual beings.

When people develop a spiritual disposition, they become increasingly sensitive to spiritual beings. Each person has his or her own capacity to bear workload, and if the amount of work exceeds their capacity, they will face a difficult situation. In other words, when they are burdened beyond their capacity, their daily lives will start to collapse, their work will collapse, or their personality will collapse. I have seen many cases like this. Especially when spiritual matters are involved, this problem is inescapable, so please keep this in mind.

Take measures objectively and calmly when you are overburdened

Even as you lead a normal life without doing anything bad, you can come under spiritual disturbance when you are suddenly given a difficult assignment at work that is beyond your abilities and are overburdened. At such times, you will be perplexed and feel anxious; you might even want to blame other people or the environment and to suspect others of conspiring against you or trying to drive you into a corner.

Others may be overburdened by the problems at home, although their coworkers may not realize it. For example, things may not be going well with their spouse, they may not have been able to sleep because they had to take care of their newborn baby, or they are constantly in an argument with their spouse over household chores. There may well be various other reasons.

When you notice that the load you carry will soon exceed your capacity, you need to look at your current work objectively and calmly, take measures to ease your burden, and make arrangements ahead of time. If there is no way you can reduce your burden, you must first abandon your perfectionism. Trying to be perfect all the time will make you overburdened by the workload, and you might end up collapsing under the weight.

The weight one can bear differs from person to person. For example, this lecture was given in front of a small audience, but an audience of the same size can be overwhelming for some speakers. If they are asked to make a speech on the same topic for about an hour, they will quickly come under negative spiritual influence and may only be able to talk about their current state of being under spiritual disturbance and how they can potentially overcome it.

People usually make excuses when they are overburdened

One can quickly become overburdened beyond one's capacity. To take an example from the earlier case, there may be various reasons for people to not be able to give a speech; they may not have done enough preparation, may have nothing substantial to talk about, may lack experience, or may not have enough spiritual abilities. Some may say, "I haven't studied enough" or "There wasn't enough time for me to prepare."

The same is true for taking a test at school. When you find an exam too difficult, you will begin to feel anxious, get flustered, and be afraid of the bad score you might receive. There are people who become too overwhelmed by difficult school exams or entrance exams and end up giving them up.

At such times, some will utterly fail, be crushed, and end up becoming a loser. Others may run away ahead of time and avoid facing the challenge. The latter will always find or create excuses to make sure they do not have to confront the challenge. I think many of their grandfathers and grandmothers have been considered "dead" in their excuses. For example, they would say, "My grandmother suddenly collapsed from a heart attack," "My grandfather just died," or "My father got into a car accident" and make up excuses for not being able to do something. Many people have probably come up with such reasons.

When people are faced with a challenge that is beyond their capacity, they will think of reasons that would allow them to avoid the challenge and put the blame on other factors. They do so because they do not want to crash head-on, just like the loser who swerves first in a game of chicken, where competitors drive toward each other on a collision course.

In the case of taking an exam, the students could say, "I failed the exam because my parents could not pay for my private tutoring school," "I couldn't go to the school of my first choice because it was far away from my home," or "We had no money to attend that school." There are various excuses like this to justify their failures. In general, however, when you start looking for an excuse, it usually means you have reached the limit of your capacity.

This applies not only in academics but also in sports. When middle or high school students join a sports team, the first month of practice is usually grueling for them; normally, every part of their body will hurt. They are not allowed to practice advanced skills yet and instead are told to do only the basic training, such as running, swinging *shinai* (bamboo sword) in kendo, and playing catch in baseball. And their whole body would hurt for an entire month from practicing. Because the pain is unbearable at the beginning, some newly joined members will quit after a few months. But those who can pass this initial stage will become stronger and will be able to endure the hard practices. They will then be able to move on to do more advanced drills.

I joined the kendo club during high school, and I saw many students quit during the month of June—that is, a few months after April, which is the start of the school year in Japan. Around that time of the year, it starts getting hotter and more humid in Japan, so practicing kendo while wearing *men* (mask), *do* (torso protector), and *hakama* (kendo uniform) makes you sweat heavily. Because it is very uncomfortable and makes you feel sick, many students quit around that time. There was such a time of the year.

There are also those who always get sick or injured before a big game and do not join others in practice. People with such tendencies may be trying to protect themselves by avoiding challenges, but they need to consider what it is they are actually trying to protect.

Observe yourself and the world objectively

It is important to always observe others and see what kind of action brings about a particular result based on the law of averages. If someone who does not regularly jog suddenly decides to enter a marathon and run over 42 kilometers, it would be very challenging and become a matter of life or death for him or her. It would also be tough for someone who does not go on walks every day to suddenly climb a mountain. Furthermore, there are many people who cannot swim or those who are afraid of water. Some of them may gain the ability to swim after one serious training session, but taking the initial leap is the hardest part.

There are also people who become traumatized after failing at something and repeatedly evade situations similar to the one they failed in. For example, you may have broken up with someone you had a serious relationship with just before getting engaged or married. It would be natural to feel hurt at such a time. But if you are too pure and naïve, you could ruin the next relationship with someone else as soon as you face a similar situation even if it had been years since the first breakup.

If you broke up with the previous partner on a rainy day, you may worry that your new relationship would end again when it rains. If you broke up after going to the movies, you may feel afraid of being invited to a movie in the new relationship. Or, eating at a French restaurant could be a sign for breaking up. In this way, there are people who have wounds in their hearts and try to subconsciously destroy the relationship as a way to avoid the pain as soon as they start to experience a similar situation. There are many other similar patterns under different circumstances.

I want to say to all the people who have such tendencies, "Look around you and pay more attention to how other people in society have ultimately turned out. Does everyone succeed without any difficulties? Do you see any cases where people fail in a particular situation? What kinds of people experience failure in that situation?" I want you to train yourself to objectively observe these points.

Break down your problem into smaller tasks

When you feel like you are about to collapse from a problem that is beyond your capacity, whether it is regarding work, study, or romantic relationships, you need to understand the extent of your capacity and the limit of the load you can bear. It is important to think of ways to reduce the number of times you exceed that limit.

One way to do this is to use "the principle of subdivision." It would be overwhelming to try and complete all your work at once. Even if you had a rush job of tunneling through a mountain and constructing a road, it would be almost impossible to accomplish it in just one day; you would need a tremendous amount of power to do so. So you first need to estimate the prospective duration of the project. If you decide to complete it in about 30 days, you then need to plan how to carry out the project by breaking down the details, including the distance you would dig every day.

The same can be said of removing snow from the roof. When there is one meter (about three feet) of snow accumulated on the roof, you cannot shovel it all at once. There are even people who fall off the roof while doing so. In this case, too, the only way to go about it is to divide the area into smaller sections and shovel the snow little by little. It would be impossible to remove it all at once.

This is also true for studying; you cannot learn everything at once. You must study things little by little, as if stacking small blocks on top of one another. Then, you will gradually be able to gain abilities and master the subject without even realizing it.

On the contrary, there are people who have a habit of doing things only at the last minute and face a difficult situation. Some may say, "I was driven into a corner so I exerted myself for just one day like Superman and passed the exam," "I was successful after studying for a short amount of time," or "I studied only the parts I guessed would appear on the test and I passed." There are many people like this, but I do not trust such methods because we cannot always depend on our hunches or accomplish things in one night.

Of course, lucky events do happen occasionally. For example, you may be able to answer the part you haphazardly reviewed before the test, but this does not happen so often in life. So it is better not to rely on luck. Generally, I am the type of person who does not depend on luck; I cover all the material so I can answer questions from all sections equally well. When I cannot answer a question, I simply accept it as such.

Do not rely on the easy ways to pass an exam

I have spoken about this before: I once got lucky on the Sundai Nationwide Mock Tests for the university entrance exams. It was a test on biology, which I chose as my science elective course in high school. On the day before the exam, a few difficult test questions in the textbook caught my attention and I carefully reviewed them. Then, to my surprise, two of the questions I reviewed were on the exam. I was able to answer them because I had happened to study them just before the exam. As a result, I got full marks and was placed first in the national rankings for biology.

But such instances are only a lucky fluke that should not be trusted. Getting lucky on a mock exam most certainly means that the same thing will not happen on the actual entrance exam because you have used up all your luck. Therefore, it is nothing to be happy about. At the time, I had a strange feeling and was surprised at how I got a perfect score.

Although I did not study biology much, I got full marks because of the two test questions I happened to review the day before. This mock exam was mainly taken by students aiming to enter the University of Tokyo, and my name was clearly displayed in first place among over 8,000 students within the humanities track. I felt a little embarrassed and thought that it would have looked better if it had been in mathematics rather than biology.

Some people may feel good about luckily coming in first in a mock exam, but the same kind of fluke will not happen in the real entrance exam, so they should be more cautious and fear such luck. It only appears as a fluke because people have not studied enough; if they had prepared thoroughly for the exam, it should not have felt like luck.

There is always a possibility of being overburdened by something that is beyond one's capacity. Those who often stay awake all night to study just before the day of the exam actually are escaping from studying despite knowing it is something they have to do. This tendency to evade a challenge is commonly observed. For example, if some friends invite you to hang out when the midterm exams are nearing, you may feel like going out with them despite knowing that you must start studying before it is too late. Before the exam, you may often find yourself wandering off with your friends who say, "Let's go to the amusement arcade," "There is a good concert. Why don't we go together?" or "I found a good restaurant. They offer complimentary service right now. Let's go eat there." This commonly happens.

Even if you are not invited by your friends, you may suddenly feel like reading a novel and start reading it a week before the exam when you should be studying. This is a classic pattern to evade a challenge. This pattern has been used for over a century, but this is how you run out of time and end up rushing at the last minute. It is worth noting that everyone has a tendency to do so to a large extent.

With this in mind, you need to think about how best to reduce the amount of pressure you feel on the exam day. You can do this by evenly breaking down the preparation you must do and taking a rational approach to succeed in your tests. Even if you were to fail, it is important to estimate beforehand how much more effort you should have put in and anticipate a possible failure so that it does not become a matter of life or death for you. There are things you can see more clearly if you look at them with the eyes of God.

Train yourself to work at a constant pace

According to what I have observed, people increasingly come under spiritual disturbance by being overwhelmed by the burden that exceeds their capacity, especially after they start working in society. Some people get overburdened when they cannot handle multiple tasks at once or when they are assigned a task with a deadline. There are also others who come under negative spiritual influence when they face something that makes them nervous— for example, a speech contest or being cast in a play.

At such times, it is important to practice thoroughly, assess what abilities you have on average, and perceive the possibility of succeeding based on your current abilities. In other words, it is important to know your "batting average," just like a professional baseball player who knows his yearly batting average despite any slumps he may experience.

If you think too highly of yourself, you tend to talk big, brag about being capable of doing something you actually are not, oversell yourself, or become conceited. As a result, you may end up ruining yourself, running away at the last minute, or causing others much trouble.

To overcome your problems, it is much better to diligently make a tangible effort to solve them. But some people neglect this effort and frequently talk to others about their worries. They go to different people and talk about their problems, only to waste their time in this way. There are people who confess their worries to someone all night and keep talking until dawn, dragging the listener into having the same worries as well.

Instead of doing this, they should practice a little more, study to gain basic knowledge, repeat drills until they can master them, or memorize their lines for a play. If you are drawing, you can study how a skilled artist draws. There are many methods to overcome your problems. It is better to efficiently use the time you have at hand little by little and work hard to make progress, even if it is a single step forward.

Even for me, if I were asked to publish 100 books a year and to write them all at once, I would not be able to do so. That is an impossible request. Even if I were asked to write 10 or at least eight books each month to produce 100 books a year, that number still feels like a stretch. But if you train yourself to work at a constant pace every day, every week, and every month and you make progress little by little, you will find yourself completing a similar amount of work by the end of the year. Therefore, it is important to train yourself while always keeping in mind your "batting average," to keep moving forward without aiming for perfection, and to produce a positive result no matter how small it may be.

The importance of perceiving your probability of success

Spiritual disturbance is generally caused by worries, suffering, or conflicting emotions. These worries and anxieties attract various beings, such as animal spirits or human spirits that are lost in hell after death. At such times, you need to perceive whether the problem you have can be solved by subdivision or through effort, as I just mentioned. But if it is something you cannot overcome, it is also important to admit that it is beyond your capacity.

When you see the limit of your capacity, decide how far you can work and how much you cannot handle. If you are dealing with tasks that must be accomplished as an organization that you belong to, you might have to suggest changing the approach, creating a short-term plan, simplifying the task, or finding someone more competent to join the team. Sometimes, taking a rest can be an important way to solve a problem. You need to change your ways of thinking in this way.

If you are under a certain amount of pressure for a prolonged period of time, your personality will truly start to disintegrate. If this happens during childhood, one can develop a complex that is difficult to be removed even after reaching adulthood, as explained by Sigmund Freud and other psychologists. Even after becoming an adult, you can develop new traumas from experiencing failure. So it is important to always be aware of your abilities from an objective perspective and carefully observe others' capabilities as well.

Ultimately, you need to foresee the probability of your success when taking on some kind of work. In a marathon of 10,000 people, for instance, the chances of coming in first would generally be one in 10,000. If you are faster than the average runner, you are likely to place in the top half. A guest runner will most likely place among the top runners. At a professional level, the slight changes in condition on the day of the race may also influence one's performance, which is another difficult factor.

Therefore, it is important to objectively look at yourself, understand your average abilities, and use "the principle of subdivision" and other ways to avoid being overburdened and burning out as much as possible. You need to do this skillfully; otherwise, there would be no end to your spiritual disturbance.

3

Self-Discipline to Avoid Coming under Spiritual Disturbance

You will lose control of your body under severe spiritual disturbance

Much like the snow accumulating on the roof, spiritual disturbance can cause the entire "house" to collapse if it becomes too severe. When this happens, the body can no longer serve as a proper "home" for the soul. Because the soul cannot reside there, it starts to go in and out of the body while still being connected to it by the silver cord. Meanwhile, this allows other spirits to freely enter the body. When spiritual disturbance becomes this serious, it is very difficult to overcome it.

In essence, the soul must have the strongest power over its body. But when the "house" has broken pillars, shattered windows, and holes in the roof, it does not properly function as a residence for the soul. Even though the soul is still connected to the body by the silver cord, the soul can hardly control the body in a situation where other spirits are going in and out of the body freely. Under these circumstances, it becomes unclear who or what is talking because the other spirits may be the ones that are inside the person's body and speaking through his or her mouth.

When listening to others talking, too, it may not be the person who is listening but something else. If things go this far, the person will start having many experiences where they do not remember things, including what they have done. Although the person has no memory of hearing something or doing something, everyone else keeps telling him or her that that was what happened, so the person begins to doubt the world and say everyone is wrong.

In medical terms, this condition is often diagnosed as dissociative disorder. There are truly cases where a person impulsively murders someone while his or her body is being taken over by a different soul. In such cases, the soul of the person is absent and the soul of a deceased murderer takes its place at the moment of the killing. That is why some criminals have no recollection of killing someone and insist that they do not know anything about the killing.

Uncontrolled clairaudience hinders you from studying or working

Another ability you might acquire after developing a spiritual disposition is clairaudience; you might hear the voices of various spirits through your ears. This spiritual hearing will not stop no matter how hard you try to cover your ears, and you will unexpectedly hear voices on various occasions.

Unless spiritual hearing is kept under control, it would be very difficult to work or study. If a student were to keep hearing a lot of voices during a test, he or she would hardly be able to pass the test. To solve this problem, some people may have no choice but to continuously listen to the CD recording of my recitation of "The True Words Spoken By Buddha" (Happy Science's basic sutra) on their headphones for 24 hours. This must be a very difficult situation.

Some people can see ghosts at all times. This, too, is a difficult situation. In general, ghosts are not supposed to be seen or heard and, fortunately, most people do not see or hear them. This is partly why people are losing faith, but being able to see various spirits is also a problem.

There are cases when people truly see the spirits that have come near them, but there are also cases when they see illusions of various things that they imagine out of fear. Fear sometimes creates illusions, making you believe they are real. This happens because you have completely lost the serenity of mind. So, in general, people who are able to see or hear spirits can be in a bad condition and be sent to a psychiatric ward.

Lead a regular lifestyle and strengthen your body, intellect, reasoning, and willpower

What, then, is necessary to prevent this worst-case scenario from happening? This is a really important point, and my advice for this is to lead a regular lifestyle as much as possible. In addition to leading a regular lifestyle, it is important to regularly train your body. Do not forget to exercise. Even horses will no longer be able to run if they stop training. So it is essential to train your physical body. If you are exerting yourself too much to meet a tight schedule, it is important to rest. You need to take a break from time to time.

There are probably people who suffer the aforementioned symptoms, such as hearing many voices of spirits, seeing various illusions, or being unable to see the world clearly, as if being covered by a veil. But these people, in particular, need to strengthen their intellect and reasoning. In addition to strengthening intellect and reasoning, it is important to train their willpower. Willpower does not become strong all of a sudden, but it will get stronger over time as you continue to train it day after day.

Because I am the kind of person who reads many books, some critics say that the spiritual messages I publish must be fabricated. They make such comments because they do not understand what I mean when I say, "An empty sack cannot stand upright." Some people believe they would be able to do work even if they were "empty" inside, as long as the spirits are there to give them instructions. But these types of people will eventually be manipulated by the spirits, lose themselves, and end up being unable to even understand what they themselves are doing.

In short, when you become able to channel spirits, it is all the more important to have substantial amount of knowledge and a properly functioning balancer between spiritual and worldly matters. There are many different ways of thinking for humans, and knowledge about the possible ways of thinking will help you to avoid being manipulated by the spirits.

Understand the law of cause and effect and be intellectual and rational

It is also very important to understand how things normally turn out based on the law of cause and effect. This, too, has to do with one's ability to reason.

When one's basic intellect does not extend beyond the level of mere superstition, the person will straightforwardly accept everything the spirits say. Those who do not understand the law of cause and effect are not rational, and these people can end up doing something terrible. For example, a person may hear the voice of a spirit saying, "If you jump off the top of this building, you will be free of pain and you can return to heaven," or "You are an angel, so even if you jump off the roof of the building, other angels will come save you by carrying you in their wings."

In American mental hospitals, when patients claim to be the reincarnation of famous people, apparently, the name "Jesus Christ" is mentioned most often. This is quite a difficult situation. They hear a spirit coming to them saying, "You are Jesus Christ." This is truly a delicate and difficult matter. I can understand how they may want to believe it to be true, but they should at least know what kind of person Jesus Christ was. They should deeply study about how Jesus lived, what thoughts he had, and how he is described in the Gospels. Whether or not they understand how Jesus would act in certain situations is crucial.

They may insist, "I already understand Jesus without studying the Bible; I am Jesus himself and will do the work of Jesus," but they will never know what is inside their "empty sack"; it could just be a "cat" going wild in that "empty sack." For this reason, once you start to develop spiritual powers, paradoxically, it is very important to be intellectual and rational.

Developing spiritual abilities means you have higher sensibility and spiritual intuition. Normally, when you have stronger inclinations toward intellect and reasoning, you become less susceptible to inspiration, tend to lose faith, and repel spiritual matters. But when you start to hear, see, and sense spiritual beings, you must devote yourself to cultivating deeper insight as a human. Otherwise, when you are given greater responsibilities or become more influential, you will be overburdened beyond your capacity and will begin to collapse.

There is no problem when you are simply sharing your spiritual experiences with your friends, jokingly telling them about a spirit that visited you and what it said. Some actors occasionally talk about their experiences of seeing dwarves or encountering ghosts on a filming trip. It is fine as long as they talk about such stories in their dressing room, but if they start to constantly talk about such spiritual experiences and can no longer draw a clear line between work and spiritual matters, then the situation is more serious.

So once you have developed a spiritual disposition, you must also strengthen your intellect and reasoning; otherwise, you cannot protect yourself in the end. Your "breakwater" is highly likely to be broken, so you need to work on building your intellectual power and your power of reasoning.

You must think intellectually and rationally, and if you find something to be impossible from the perspective of the law of cause and effect no matter how hard you think, you must reject it boldly and decisively, as if cutting it off with a short sword. For example, if a spirit is telling you to jump off from the top of the mountain because an angel will come to save you, you must be able to refute it by saying, "This must be the devil's whisper." You need to at least know that the devils are usually the ones to say such things.

Even if the pope thinks he needs to have similar abilities as Jesus and tries to walk on water in a swimming pool, he will most likely end up instantly sinking. In this case, one should know the difference between oneself and Jesus. Miracles do occur at times, but even miracles must be perceived with a certain calmness.

You can ward off the temptations of the spirits by continuously studying the Truth

There are other points I want you to be careful of. When you have spiritually awakened, become increasingly sensitive to spiritual matters, or become more susceptible to spiritual influence, it will become easier for various spirits to take over your personality. So it is extremely important to make serious efforts to be a good person and improve your character as a human being. Even in regard to the words you speak, it is important to make an effort to use good words and avoid rude words that may hurt others. Of course, it is also wrong to use violence, even though you may want to justify it as God's punishment.

There are people who actively deceive others, lie, or cheat. Some people are even worse; they plot to make others fall into a trap and gradually lead them to their downfall. Rather than impulsively lying or cheating, they purposefully try to destroy or trip others and drive them into a corner. Some deceive ignorant people who would easily jump on a sweet deal and form a group with them to drive someone to destruction. There are various cases, so I advise that you also develop intellectual power and power of reasoning as much as possible so you can fight off the traps that have been set.

There are certainly times when God or Buddha will save you, but you cannot expect to receive help all the time. If you and your actions are inviting negative incidents, the consequences will eventually come back to you. Therefore, you must be strong against any trap for your downfall.

Once people start to hear the voices of spirits, some of them believe 100 percent of what the spirits say, but the spirits are not always right. Happy Science publishes many books on Buddha's Truth, so I hope you will continue to study the Truth. The spirits that have been in hell or on the rear side of the spirit world[1] for a long time, in particular, have not studied the Truth very much. So your attitude to keep studying the Truth will help ward off their words and temptations to a certain extent.

In fact, their words are not completely opposite to the Truth; they twist the Truth very slightly and insert fallacies in their words. For example, they may say, "Love is important, right? So, when practicing love, all that matters is knowing how to seduce others. You need to improve the skills to lure others into loving you." Others may use alcohol and say, "Alcohol is also a useful catalyst to get on well with others." They may excessively flatter or lie and trick someone in many ways to make the person lose confidence or believe he or she is no good.

People with extreme mood swings must work to maintain a stable mind

Some people have a manic-depressive temperament and tend to experience extreme moods and periodically go between sadistic and masochistic states. People with this tendency are more likely to come under spiritual disturbance, allowing many spirits to freely enter these people. Extreme mood swings allow spirits to very easily enter the minds of people, so it is important to maintain a stable mind.

What would happen if you leave this tendency as it is and consider it as acceptable? If it becomes your habit to severely accuse or abuse others, the habit will become part of your personality. On the contrary, if you have a tendency to badly torture yourself by focusing on proving how worthless you are and "enjoy" doing so every day, then you would also be beyond help.

Therefore, if you have these tendencies, make an effort to develop the power of reasoning and view things based on a general, statistical perspective—that is, how people of a certain sex, age, educational background, career, and family structure usually think—although spiritual people may not like this approach. Those with extreme mood swings are generally vulnerable to spiritual influence, so I advise them to make an effort to maintain a stable mind as much as possible.

4

A Mirror-like Mind That Repels Curses

Those who stray from the group are easily targeted

Once you have developed a spiritual disposition and start to channel spirits, it is difficult to undo your ability to channel spirits in most cases. But the study of the Truth, faith, and your Dharma friends will protect you under such conditions. You will truly be protected by being part of the group of people with faith. Please know that those who stray from the group can easily be targeted.

The mass media often mock and look down on faith and insist that they will not believe what is not visible to the naked eye. When they see believers worshipping or gathering to study the Truth at churches or temples, they say the people are all brainwashed and confuse people. But having friends with similar faith is crucial in protecting yourself from being completely defeated by the devils. One of the methods devils take to attack people is to make them stray from the group so that they become a lone wolf. So please be wary of this tactic.

People mainly stray from the group because they think too highly of themselves and are too conceited, have tendencies to talk big or lie, have too strong desire for fame, or are too proud.

They may certainly have various traits others might praise; they may be smart, attractive, have been born with a good family lineage or into a wealthy family, have a nice house, have a great career, have respectful ancestors, or have excellent children. They may have qualities that are superior to others. However, if they become too proud of themselves and start to believe they are different from everyone else, they will end up standing out in the crowd and become an easy target to shoot down.

For this reason, it is important to stay humble and continue making steady efforts. Even if you occasionally succeed, become popular with people, or produce good results, it is best to tell yourself that you were just lucky this time and that things will not always go so well.

Do not dwell on the glories of your past but expand the scope of your responsibilities

The same is often said about university entrance exams. When I enrolled in university, one of the professors told us something along the lines of, "You all have passed the exams to enter this university, but only less than 20 percent of you here would be able to pass the same exams one year later. This is how things are, so don't assume you have earned a solid position or status. You have succeeded this time, but it was probably because you luckily studied the material that happened to appear in the exams. Remember, 80 percent of you will fail if you were to take the exams again next year."

In that sense, you may have succeeded in the exams simply because you were lucky. You may, of course, feel confident about having passed the exams; but instead of thinking you have crossed the finish line, it is important to remain humble and keep making efforts after that.

Those who dwell on the glories of their past tend to remain immature and avoid new challenges. Around the time of their graduation, for example, they may avoid finding a job or making decisions about their future. Some may continue to depend on their parents and put off making commitments.

Therefore, it is important to mature appropriately with age; you must be able to take care of yourself on your own and start bearing responsibilities for others as well. You need to be responsible for your family, including your spouse, children, parents, and siblings. At work, you need to be responsible for your colleagues and subordinates. You also need to be responsible for your neighbors or in fulfilling the role you are given in society. In this way, the scope of your responsibilities must expand. To do this, it is important to expand your capacity by building upon the abilities you now have through steady efforts and become capable of doing more things.

Precepts are like fences to prevent you from falling off a cliff

Precepts or disciplines that have been set in place since ancient times do not necessarily guarantee your success even if you observed all of them. Many of them were set based on general tendencies that led people to failure. For example, some religions forbid consuming alcohol because countless people have failed due to their drinking habits.

"You shall not kill" is another common rule because there is almost nothing good about killing. But there are times when killing can be justified. People in the military sometimes have to kill people to fulfill their duty. Some police officers may have killed criminals when they exchanged fire. Even so, taking even one life can be hard on one's conscience; even if the police officers were admired for their skills after killing many criminals, they may gradually feel like visiting a church to pray. It is understandable that they feel this way.

Various precepts or disciplines that exist are like fences that prevent you from falling off a cliff. With this in mind, you need to think about how best to live your life in your current position.

Ikiryo *can be repelled by* "*the law of the mirror*"

There are cases in which your life goes wrong due to a spiritual cause; someone's *ikiryo* (spirit of a living person) may come to possess you, or a person who often sends his or her *ikiryo* may dispatch his or her spiritual "minions" to attack you. Many people actually experience failure as a result of being spiritually attacked by others or being at the receiving end of someone's grudge, so please be careful.

In principle, if your mind has been polished like a shiny mirror, these negative thoughts will bounce back to the person who emitted them. But if you stand on the same playing field as the other person, their "punches" can hit you, though you may also be able to "punch" the other person. So you need to strive to not stand on the same playing ground. As long as you keep your "mirror" clean, negative thoughts will be repelled.

Some people send their *ikiryo* or the "minions" of their *ikiryo*—the equivalent of *shikigami* that *Onmyoji* (Yin-Yang Masters) use—to spiritually attack other people, so it is necessary to master the art of repelling spirits. The art of repelling spirits means creating a state of mind that allows you to become one with God or Buddha and maintaining a mind that is as calm as the surface of a still lake or as clean as a polished mirror.

A polished mirror will show the devil-like image of the other person or the person turning into an animal and trying to attack you. So, in principle, you need to create a mirror-like mind that will reflect the other person's desires to inflict pain on you, lead you to ruin, or destroy your life. Then you will be able to repel those negative thoughts. So polish your mind until you can do this. Amaterasu-O-Mikami, or the Sun Goddess, is often symbolized by a circular mirror; this represents the teaching, "Create a mirror-like mind." As long as you maintain a mirror-like mind, you will not be continuously affected by the delusive thoughts that may be directed at you.

If you are under constant attack from someone's delusive thoughts but cannot move away from that environment, efforts must be made to resolve the problem. In such cases, someone needs to confront that person about the problem and point out the mistakes in his or her ways of thinking. But, in general, you can repel most negative thoughts with "the law of the mirror." This is how I usually fight.

In real life, you can be the target of various aggressive thoughts or evil thoughts, so there are times when you have to logically refute their points and fight back to counter their attack. You may sometimes have to do it as part of your job. Otherwise, you may need to repel any negative thoughts with a mirror-like mind so that the seeds of hatred will not be planted in your mind. It is as if you are commanding the *ikiryo*, "Go back to the one who has sent you." It is extremely important to repel others' grudges, suspicions, or curses to kill or destroy you in this way.

5

Grow as a Human and Enhance Your Ability

Be strong in long-lasting fights as well

I have discussed the topic of recovering from spiritual disturbance. During the process of growing as a human and achieving self-realization in the truest sense of the word, you will develop abilities as a person and start to demonstrate greater strengths than others. When there is a large disparity between your overall abilities as a human and those of your opponent, you will no longer have to fight to win. So, fundamentally, it is essential to work on enhancing your abilities further, one step at a time.

Regarding larger issues involving the entire society, there is not much you can do as an individual. But times of hardship do not usually last long. So each person needs to think about how to persevere during such times and skillfully shield oneself or take shelter in a "turtle's shell" until the difficult times pass. For example, even if an economic recession were to occur, it will not last forever. So it is important to be creative and find ways to live through it.

Those who easily come under spiritual disturbance tend to think about the short-term and decide to take action based on short-term perspectives, but they must be strong in long-lasting fights as well. As they persist, they may find that they have significantly grown without even realizing it. And when they are no longer an "empty sack," they will notice that the opponent they were facing is nowhere to be found. Therefore, when you have become the target of negative thoughts, it is all the more important to remind yourself that your efforts, achievements, and virtue are still far from satisfactory and to work on building them up.

Your road is endless, so keep wishing to advance your work and life

There is a matter of compatibility in all relationships, so you may also encounter those you find it difficult to get along with. This cannot be helped. You cannot always be loved by everyone. Even Jesus Christ, who taught love, was not loved by all people; he also encountered adversaries at the time. Therefore, we cannot be loved by everyone.

Especially when a different sense of values is involved, you may face more adversaries. At such times, it is important to live as sincerely as possible and repel what needs to be repelled. There are things you can refute and those you cannot. But it is essential to clearly point out the mistakes in others' deeds in light of God's

Will. When I am confronted by various *ikiryo* or evil spirits, I sometimes converse with them to drive them away, but there are times when talking is not enough to dispel them. At such times, I draw in the flash of lightning from heaven—like an electric shock—to expel them.

Your road is endless and is probably difficult. However, keep wishing to advance your work and life. I believe such an attitude is essential. It is also important to be determined to not allow evil actions to be committed beyond a certain level.

In this chapter, I have spoken about recovering from spiritual disturbance. There may be times when you have to confront people who are under spiritual disturbance and times when you yourself come under spiritual disturbance. You need to think about how to take precautions in both cases. I shared some of my thoughts in a general way based on my own experiences. I hope they will be of some help to you in the future.

CHAPTER THREE

The Condition of the Real Exorcist

The Spiritual Initiation on Exorcism

Originally recorded in Japanese on February 6, 2020,
at the Special Lecture Hall of Happy Science in Japan,
and later translated into English.

1

The Essence of Exorcists

Whether you know the secrets of the inner world
makes a big difference

In connection to the theme of this chapter, I have already published a book called *The Real Exorcist* (New York: IRH Press, 2020). I have also published two of my English lectures, *The Real Exorcist* and *How to Create the Spiritual Screen*, along with their Japanese translations.[2] Because I have already given many teachings on this topic, some of the points I make here may overlap, but I decided to talk about this topic again to add greater depth to it.

With that said, it is extremely difficult to talk about this topic in words; the true meaning of my words may not necessarily reach everyone's heart. There are certain things that can only be understood through actual experience. In Zen Buddhism, there is a saying that enlightenment cannot be expressed through words, and this topic may be of this kind. Some people may instantaneously understand it, whereas others may not, no matter how many times it is explained to them.

In a sense, this topic belongs to the world of spiritual training and the realm of experts, so people's abilities and state of mind make a big difference. In the world of swordsmanship, masters can instantly understand their opponents' abilities just by looking at them and without actually fighting them with a sword. Your state of mind determines the area of the spirit world you are connected to, so how you attune your mind to heaven and repel evil is especially important.

The world of the mind is truly mystical. One's mind can immediately be attuned to someone on the other side of the globe or even into the vast universe. Once you understand the secrets of the inner world, you will know that the mind can truly expand infinitely, like opening one's hand, and it can contract to a single point, like closing one's hand. Contracting to a point and expanding to infinity—that is what it feels like.

I have been working in religion for decades, but I still have many experiences that give me a sense of wonder. When I read books on exorcists and watch movies on exorcism, I often find their depictions to be very different from what I experience, although there are similarities at times. In fact, there is a tremendous gap between the works created based solely on imagination and those based on real knowledge gained through experience.

So no matter how many times I expound on this topic, I am afraid my teachings will not reach people beyond a certain level; this is not possible unless people have grasped the teachings as the truth in their minds or through experience. For some people, these teachings may be beyond their reach forever.

THE LAWS OF SECRET

Always polishing the qualities that put off devils

As you study and undergo spiritual training at Happy Science, you may become spiritually sensitive and develop a spiritual disposition to some extent. When you are in a good state of mind, you may sometimes be able to communicate with your guardian and guiding spirits or expel evil spirits. However, this also depends on the spirits you are dealing with.

When you have not sufficiently awakened or gained spiritual awareness, far superior archangels, great tathagatas, or god-like beings will not normally come to you. But if you think too highly of yourself, become conceited, and have too much pride at this stage, you may begin to feel as if you yourself are a great god, tathagata, or bodhisattva and mistakenly believe that you are connected to such beings despite the lack of spiritual training. When this happens, the good spirits that have been coming to you will be replaced by the bad ones before you realize it, and you may end up straying from the path and being manipulated by invisible beings.

There are many people who work as spiritual mediums or have founded small religious groups with this level of spiritual awareness. But usually, the principle of democracy is at work, and even if they were to carry out activities in the same way as the service industry, it is difficult for them to have a large number of followers. Because everyone can more or less sense whether something is spiritually pleasant or unpleasant, people will eventually distance themselves from the mediums or groups that have come under negative spiritual influences and are constantly affected by evil spirits.

However, some of them still attract many people for specific reasons. They gather people who want to fulfill particular needs, such as seeking divine favors or forgiveness for their sins. At such places, it is possible for someone controlled by what Happy Science sees as wicked spirits to have an influence over a large number of people or to run an organization of a certain size. We need to be wary of this.

Ultimately, the condition of the real exorcist comes down to whether you can coexist with others when your true nature as well as the true natures of others are exposed. For example, would you be able to keep company with other people if you can read their thoughts and feelings and have them read yours while you live and work in society or even when meeting with customers in the drawing room? If you find it impossible to associate with them, cannot bear to even be in the same space, wish they would not come the next day, or hope you would never see them again, then you will not be able to meet them anymore. That is the reality.

Therefore, although there are different ways to describe exorcists, the essence of exorcists lies in their attitude to always polish the qualities that put off devils. This is the difficult part.

2

The Conditions for Humans to Survive and the Conditions for the Devils to Attack

Fasting makes it easier to be attuned to human or animal spirits that starved to death

To live and survive in this three-dimensional world, or the material world, certain conditions must be met. No one can evade all the conditions. We all live under certain conditions. For example, we cannot live without eating or drinking water. We cannot live without having relationships with others at all. In modern society, we also need financial strength and may want a place to live, whether it is a house, a condo, or an apartment. Furthermore, we need an environment to continue working, and we need to maintain a healthy body and prevent illnesses or disabilities that will hinder us from working.

Our optimal survival is only possible when our lives are supported by certain conditions. But some of the conditions that allow us to live and survive in this world overlap and cannot be separated from the conditions for the devils to attack. For example, fasting is sometimes practiced in religion, but in reality, it is very difficult for someone who has fasted for a week to summon high spirits, be attuned to them, and communicate with them. Such a person is most probably preoccupied with the thought of food, so it is more likely for him or her to attract beings that share a similar state of mind.

Many animals have such a state of mind. In the mountains and forests, many wild animals starve to death during the harsh winter season, when there is little food. They experience the fear of dying from lack of food. So the minds of those who practice fasting can sometimes be attuned to these animal spirits.

There are also human spirits who suffered through a similar situation. For example, many people died during the war because they continued fighting despite the severe shortages of food. This kind of suffering is not so easy to overcome. Of course, this state of suffering will not last very long for those who had some knowledge about the world of Truth and were able to accept their deaths. But the spirits of those who have yet to understand that they have died will continue to suffer and can be drawn to people who practice fasting.

In particular, practitioners of ascetic training who seclude themselves in the mountains and carry out circumambulation or fast will easily be approached by the spirits of those who died while undergoing similar training. But in the beginning, they may feel as if they are hearing the voices of god, buddha, bodhisattvas, or tathagatas. An extreme situation or a significant lack of something causes you to fixate on one thought, so you need to be careful. I believe Shakyamuni Buddha taught the Middle Way because he deeply understood such dangers through his own experience.

The relationship between the condition of the real exorcist and financial status

Many religions have a long history, and many of them teach the idea of honorable poverty. I am not necessarily opposed to this idea; I rather think it is good to practice this idea to some extent while one undergoes spiritual discipline.

Nowadays, many people raise issues about economic disparity and poverty. From an objective perspective, we can say that those who have experienced extreme poverty and lack of material goods or money during their childhood or adolescence are more likely to be involved in the world of crime. It is also common for them to envy the wealthy. So it is important to strive to attain a certain level of economic stability.

Deficiency justifies all actions, even if they are crimes. Big cities such as Tokyo are abundant with things, and if you are walking on the streets penniless or extremely hungry, you might think that stealing a little from those who have more than enough would not be a problem. It is understandable for one to feel that way. There are also movies and TV dramas that justify such actions. This is certainly a difficult issue, but we need to know that these actions are by no means heavenly.

On the contrary, people living in abundance of money because they have successful and wealthy parents, were born into a family of landowners, or belong to a big financial group can easily be corrupted. If children are raised in material abundance, they can become corrupted. If they are raised in an environment with excess money, they might become unable to understand what it means to work to earn money. They might develop the tendency to always expect help from others and become dependent on them. They might also tend to look down on and make fun of the poor or people with regular jobs. Unfortunately, there are also dangerous sides to being wealthy.

As for myself, I had quite a normal life in my childhood and adolescent years. I learned Benjamin Franklin's idea that "time is money" and made an effort to effectively spend my time so that I can convert time into financial gain. Through such efforts, I deeply learned the importance of earning money to pay for one's living expenses, education, and books to study from.

But even though I lived with those thoughts in mind, it was not until I was 30 years old that I finally managed to move out of a rented studio apartment of about 10 square meters (108 square feet). I only had a certain amount of space to store the books I bought, and there was a limit to the number of books I could buy. Because I had limited space and money, I thought I must read all the books I bought.

The situation may be different for those who can afford to buy any book they want. For example, if someone inherited a fortune of millions of dollars upon his or her parents' death, that person can buy a spacious condo and as many books as he or she wants. The person can look at him or herself as an intellectual or pretend to be one just by lining up these books.

There certainly are people who have succeeded in quickly gaining academic status with their wealth. There are cases where people have become scholars more quickly than others due to the "intellectual stock" accumulated from their parents' and grandparents' generations as a family of scholars. Sometimes wealth can work positively in this way. But there are others who become mere dilettantes or pretentious people and show off their knowledge. What they learn will not necessarily lead them to cultivate a truly virtuous character or to make any contributions or improvements to society. This is also the difficult part. Because all things have both positive and negative sides to them, we must be careful.

Some people who financially struggle every day may endure poverty and keep working hard to move forward little by little, as if to say, "Heaven be my witness." If these people make convincing efforts that even others would approve of, there should be very little chance for them to become agents of evil. However, if they develop resentment, jealousy, anger, or criminal tendencies as they struggle, they could turn to crime or delinquency at a young age or in their late teens. There are cases where such juvenile delinquents band together to commit crimes. Taking these possibilities into consideration, experiencing extreme poverty for a prolonged period of time to the extent of distorting one's human nature is not a favorable condition for becoming the real exorcist.

Devils attack your wounds from the past or troubles with the opposite sex

Historically, when founders of religions awakened to their calling, poverty, serious illnesses, or the death of a parent often worked as catalysts for them to enter the path of religion or the road to enlightenment. So we cannot know the end result unless we see things from a long-term perspective. But objectively speaking, people face powerful headwind when they are driven toward a corrupt, crime-ridden environment, and it takes considerable resolve and abilities to advance forward under such circumstances.

Experiencing financial or economic struggles, ill-health due to sicknesses or disabilities, or illnesses or deaths in the family can distort people's minds and make them unable to get back on their feet or to rebuild their lives. In reality, there are people who have lost one or both of their parents during childhood. However, not everyone becomes a criminal after going through such a misfortune. Some manage to overcome it, build a happy family, and have a decent job, whereas others use the misfortune as an excuse to become a bad person. We must be careful regarding this point.

When going into battle with a devil, you may sometimes find "thorns" or "needles" that have been stuck at the roots of your soul or in the history of your life. These thorns or needles are hard to remove, so the devils may take advantage of them to approach you. You may think that these experiences are all in the past. But if the thorns are still stuck in your mind, devils can use these thorns to sneak into your mind. So you need to be careful.

For this reason, you must practice self-reflection very deeply. You need to polish and purify your mind by tracking back all the events of the past, checking how you reacted to and handled each of them, and examining what thoughts you had at the time. Otherwise, even if you may appear to be doing well in dealing with devils at first, as you continue to fight more devils, you will eventually face stronger ones that will fight as if to stab a knife into the wounds of your past.

The same can be said about issues involving romantic relationships. It is very rare to find a person who has never been hurt in a relationship with the opposite sex. At one point or another, everyone gets hurt, becomes heartbroken, breaks someone's heart, or fails at relationships; some relationships may have been ruined due to a family issue, financial problems, or academic matters. Many people have probably developed new karma as a result of issues involving romantic relationships.

In a sense, most people get caught up with such issues in one way or another. It is unusual if you have not been "caught" like the fish in a fishing pond once or twice; you may recall the pain of the scar from being hooked or getting a hook in the cheek when you thought you were biting into a piece of food. I think everyone has, at least slightly, experienced such pain. Although some people may have forgotten about them, these experiences can shape one's tendencies of the soul.

In fact, such relationship issues involving the opposite sex can be a very big problem in the world of spiritual mediumship, especially when exorcisms are involved. This is because these issues are often used as one of the largest targets for the devils to attack. They are hard to solve; you may be able to solve the problem when it only concerns you, but when another person is involved in interpersonal relationships, things get extremely difficult.

Those who are on the road to enlightenment must fear the dangers of getting tripped by relationships

Let me explain this in a simple way. When you are working toward a particular goal—in academic studies, study of Buddha's Truth, or spiritual training, for instance—you may have someone nearby who unconditionally loves you and encourages you. This person's love and encouragement can work like a strong buoyant force to help you move forward. In many cases, the presence of such a person can positively work in this way and can help you be stronger than when you are fighting alone.

However, there are of course times when such relationships fall apart. The person who has been supporting you and providing you with the power to move forward can turn into the seed of trouble for you to trip over. This is especially true when you are undergoing religious training.

After all, everyone has their own self-interests and thinks about their gains and losses. As long as your interests—such as carrying out spiritual discipline, studying Buddha's Truth, and devoting yourself to the Truth or your studies—match the interests of the other person, things will go well. But there can be times when your interests conflict, and that is when the relationship can fall apart beyond repair.

For example, a young woman may fall in love with a man who is working hard to study the Truth and their relationship may start off well. Her family may also welcome the young man because he seems to be an outstanding individual. However, her parents may have their own interests as medical practitioners and expect the young man to go to medical school and become a doctor. They may even want the two to be an ideal couple who could take over their business. If they had such desires, problems could arise as soon as the young man takes a different path. This may even cause his relationship with the young woman to fail in the end.

The same thing can happen to those whose parents are lawyers, judges, or other judicial officers. The parents may approve their son's or daughter's partner while he or she is a law school student, but if the partner chooses a completely different career path, factors that were once positive may start to have a negative influence on the relationship.

There may also be someone who had not thought much about his or her future career but later starts to consider becoming a religious leader. What if the person has been going out with someone whose parents work in the media industry? Of course, we cannot make any sweeping conclusions because there are many types of people in the media industry, including faithful and pure-hearted people. But if the partner's parents were the type of journalists who write or report on any story that would sell, even if it were fabricated, then their relationship could soon take a turn for the worse.

Things like this can happen, and it is very difficult to escape issues involving interpersonal relationships. So those who are on the road to enlightenment must fear the dangers of getting tripped by relationships. That is why you must sometimes limit your social interactions for a certain period of time to carry out spiritual training, even if you are naturally cheerful, sociable, pleasant, positive, and able to establish good relationships with different types of people. If you openly associate with various people, you will have to adjust yourself to them, which may hinder your spiritual training. Things can get entangled even further if a romantic relationship is involved.

3

The Targets the Devils Continuously Attack until the End: The Desire for Fame and Jealousy

An example of a Happy Science supporter in its early days

It is truly sad when people who have supported you suddenly turn their backs on you, but even faithful people who believe themselves to be pure-minded have desires.

Among all the desires, which one would be left until the end? Some people may abandon worldly interests and dedicate themselves to religious activities by saying they do not care about money or staying single. However, even these people find it difficult to get rid of the desire for fame until the very end.

For example, there are people even in religious organizations who suddenly start to express rage or rise against the leader as soon as they fail to fill an honorable position. I have experienced this many times over the last 30-some years. It is unbelievable how many people get tricked so easily by this simple formula.

Although it may seem laughable to the current Happy Science believers and may even seem impossible from the perspective of the current Happy Science group, which carries out activities in more than 164 countries around the world (as of August 2021), I had the following experience in the past. In the very beginning, when I had just quit my job to launch Happy Science, I planned to start with the minimum possible capital. So I rented a 10-square-meter room in a house owned by one of the first passionate believers to use as an office. But this person had her own ideas about the scale of the Happy Science movement and believed that a small, unused room that had an outdoor staircase would be enough as our permanent office. She certainly had good intentions when she offered to rent out the space to me for free. But a religion whose main office does not expand beyond a single room would be too small.

At the time, I had just quit my job and was quite prudent. I wanted to make sure Happy Science would not close down. To tell the truth, my father and elder brother had opened a private tutoring school about a year before that, but the school was completely in the red and their imminent bankruptcy was clear. In these circumstances, I thought I should build a solid foundation and make sure not to spend too much money to start Happy Science.

Then, about six months later, we found a bigger, 55-square-meter (592-square-foot) basement office space with a rental fee of about ¥150,000 (about US$1,000 based on the exchange rate at the time) nearby in the same town. When we decided to move there, the passionate supporter who had let us use her room out of kindness started to feel offended. After all, she knew she could manage the office and expressed her opinions as long as she was renting out her room to us. However, when we moved to a bigger office, hired some staff members, and created the position of secretary general, she was no longer able to do the same. So she began to express opposition to management, causing much dispute.

After another six months, our relationship got even worse when we moved our office again to an even better space of about 90 square meters (969 square feet) located in front of the nearest railway station. Nevertheless, our relationship continued while we were still in the same town, but as soon as we moved downtown, it completely fell apart; the person not only refused to speak to us but also sent back whatever we mailed her.

I wondered why she could not understand the simple truth that Happy Science would naturally grow and expand over the course of time. I was involved in large-scale businesses while working at a company, so despite starting out small, I had intended to gradually expand Happy Science from the outset. So it was natural for me to hire more people and move to a larger office, but to her, such changes probably appeared like an act of betrayal. She then felt like she was being deceived because she had hoped to remain as a permanent leader and manager of Happy Science.

But no one would follow her. A few of her long-term friends, who had reluctantly helped her when Happy Science was just starting out, sided with her, but other than them, this issue had nothing to do with the believers who joined the organization later. A growing organization naturally requires a suitable environment for development.

At times like these, inner conflicts arise and allow the devil to enter one's mind. Even if you have been carrying out sufficient spiritual training to be able to protect yourself from the devil in your ordinary life, when the environment changes and the devil ultimately takes advantage of your desire for fame, you can come under the devil's influence.

The difficulty involving close relationships

I have experienced similar problems with my own family. I have five children, who were all raised in the same environment and were looked after by many staff members from a young age. But as Happy Science expanded and they grew older, they gradually faced a difficult situation. Because they had many staff members helping them, they may have assumed it was the staff members' job to serve them. But once they reached adulthood, they were told to go out and work like a new staff member, so some of them began to feel offended by the sudden change of treatment. It was not easy for some of them to make a fresh start.

In such cases, one must be able to understand how society works as a whole and how other people think and perceive things.

However, this type of knowledge is not taught in textbooks. Whether you can perceive these and understand the need to change your attitude depends on how sensible you are.

Relationship issues involving people you are close with, such as family members, relatives, and friends, are quite difficult to deal with. This is particularly true for romantic relationships. The example I cited earlier was my experience of starting a religion, but even if I had not started a religion and worked as an independent spiritual medium instead, I probably would have had similar problems.

Everyone has his or her own free will. Even if someone were to take pride in working close to me, being my right hand, managing Happy Science, financially supporting it as *Daikokuten* (angel of wealth), or instructing others as senior members, as the organization develops, they may eventually become unfit to fulfill their current roles and find themselves going further away from me. At such times, they often go into a rage.

I imagine that business owners who started businesses and rapidly developed their companies most probably had similar experiences. They may not be able to see the spiritual aspects, but the same thing is probably happening from an objective point of view. During times like these, problems regarding the desire for fame and jealousy will arise.

Relationships with the opposite sex will remain an eternal challenge

In the end, desires will always arise in a relationship between a man and a woman. When I first started Happy Science, I was still single. Because of this, my mother in my hometown would tell me to be cautious. She warned me that many people who worked hard to support me while I was single would suddenly change their attitude, speak behind my back, or accuse me as soon as I got married. She also advised me not to disclose the amount of money I had in my savings. Certainly, if the amount of provisions a person has is revealed, others can easily have leverage over him or her. This is all about worldly knowledge.

Just as my mother had anticipated, some supportive people around me suddenly turned critical and aggressive toward me as soon as I got married. This is indeed a difficult issue. It certainly is not easy to take an objective stance and openheartedly accept the marriage of the person you are interested in.

Such issues arise in relationships with the opposite sex, but they also occur in relationships with those of the same sex. For example, there were many men, especially among the older ones, who expressed their dissatisfaction with me marrying and having a family, saying they had come all the way to help me spread the Truth.

Relationship issues are truly difficult. Relationships with the opposite sex will most probably remain an eternal challenge.

4

Relationship between Exorcism and Issues with the Opposite Sex

Examples of food that can boost the power of exorcism

There is another big issue.

To exorcise devils in real life, one needs to have a certain amount of vitality or, more specifically, spiritual power. For example, it is often advised to eat food that boosts your energy to recover from illnesses, and people eat nutritious foods such as beefsteak and bananas to gain energy. The same can be said about exorcisms. One must be overflowing with physical power to exorcise devils and evil spirits; otherwise, the person will not have enough power to expel them. So, energy-boosting foods can be effective.

In vampire movies, we often see how vampires dislike garlic. I came to understand this notion quite well after I entered the path of religion. Because eating garlic makes one smell bad, I used to think that vampires were fleeing from the unbearable scent of garlic they smelled when sucking the blood from a person's neck. That may be true, but garlic generally gives you energy; it helps fight off viruses and heal colds. Similar effects can be found in other foods such as Chinese chives, liver, onions, and green onions. There are other foods that *sennin* use to gain energy.

There are also regular foods that give you energy, such as eel, beefsteak, and pork cutlet. Such foods fill your body with energy—the kind that makes your body hot—and give you the power to exorcise evil spirits. When you are fueled with energy, you can expel evil spirits, but when you are exhausted, you cannot. This happens in reality; exorcisms truly use the same energy.

In terms of one's physical condition, having the power to expel malicious spirits also means that one is full of vitality. It is similar to the power exerted by an athlete, a passionate salesperson, or a successful businessperson. However, following such a diet on a daily basis will also fuel strong sexual desires, which in turn will increase the risk of being tempted by the opposite sex.

Make efforts to control your sexual desires and use them for a good cause

The temptation of the opposite sex, which I greatly feared when I was young, is not the kind of danger that immediately sends you to hell as if falling down a manhole. Rather, it is more of a gradual process, like becoming entangled in a spider web little by little or dropping ink into a bucket of water one drop at a time until it can no longer be used for drinking or washing clothes. So a single experience of being trapped does not immediately cause everything to fall apart at once.

There are certainly people who completely ruin their lives because of a single encounter with the opposite sex. But this is similar to how one can suddenly get into an accident while driving a car; lack of prudence can lead to such results. In general, however, it takes time to get entangled in a spider web or to taint the water one drop of ink at a time. You will not be completely ruined right away.

When people have robust health and tremendous vitality, they will develop sexual desires and fantasies of the opposite sex. This is the difficult part. Particularly in youth, this cannot be helped. Sexual desire can become very strong when one is still not old enough to get married, so young people may sometimes have a hard time. This desire gradually subsides with age. But by the time people reach an old age, they also lose the competence to work.

There is no doubt that one is able to do much work when he or she is young and energetic. One's productive years at work usually coincide with the period when he or she is popular with the opposite sex and frequently goes out for drinks at the bars downtown. Therefore, how to manage to control such desires during this period is very important; whether or not you make efforts to convert and use them for a good cause will make a big difference.

Alcohol prevents one from repelling evil spirits or calling on high spirits

I have touched upon the subject of alcohol several times in the past. I cannot drink much, so people with genetically high tolerance for alcohol may feel the effects of alcohol a little differently than I do.

Even after I became able to channel spirits and summon high spirits at any time, I still had to go out for drinks or dinner in the evenings to fulfill my social obligations while I worked at a company. However, whenever I drank alcohol—even if I did not drink very much of it—high spirits would not respond to my call. Even if I tried to summon them after returning home, I could not connect with my own guardian spirit, let alone the high spirits I usually communicated with. It was exactly like a telephone call not going through; while alcohol remained in my body, I simply could not connect with them.

On the contrary, evil spirits and low spirits would come immediately, so I became more vulnerable to being possessed by such spirits. If I happened to visit a bad place, I even brought one home but could not dispel it in those conditions; when I consumed alcohol and was drunk, I could not expel the possessing spirit or call on the high spirits to help me expel it. This was very clear. The only thing I could do was rest until I sobered up and the alcohol was completely out of my system.

At work, social obligations were inevitable, and I had to meet with many people who were possessed by evil spirits. I had no choice at the time. I could not go elsewhere to avoid these people because it would be rude to do so. There were things I had to do because it was work.

Especially after gaining spiritual powers, I could instantly tell whether a person was possessed or even the number of spirits possessing them, so my face naturally turned pale whenever I met someone who was possessed. It was tough to spend one or two hours with such a person in that condition. It was particularly tough in the office, where the workers sat in close proximity to each other and the seats were assigned; if the person was a senior worker or manager, I definitely could not ask for a seating change because it would only look as if I disliked that person.

It was also unfortunate that I could hardly stop the interference from those spirits. Evil spirits possessing the people sitting across from, next to, or diagonally from me would talk to me during work, so it was truly unbearable. I doubt that there is anyone who can tolerate this.

When I was feeling a little off because I had a few drinks with my co-workers the night before and did not get enough sleep, it was already tough to deal with English-related tasks or to read

English documents. In addition to that, the spirits possessing the people across from me would come and talk to me. I sometimes wanted to tell the possessed people to deal with their own problems themselves. Because the spirits just kept on nagging me, there was no way I could focus on my work. So I fought to expel such spirits inside my mind as I worked.

The look on my face was probably awful when I looked at these possessed people or when our eyes met because I could see the terrible thoughts they had in their minds. I may have appeared like I could not get on well with certain types of people and was rather picky. This kind of difficulty was inevitable.

Sexuality issues in Christianity, Islam, and Buddhism

Various traditional religions have many teachings on self-control, precepts, and disciplines. These teachings were derived from experiences, so they do not necessarily apply to everyone. They were probably created to give a general warning about the most common causes of downfall or failure. So it does not necessarily mean that you will be immediately condemned for defying just one of them; they point out where people generally tend to trip.

Matters regarding sexuality will become major issues within religious circles as well; there will probably be a fierce clash of values, especially after 2020. For example, I saw some news about the 2020 U.S. Democratic Party presidential primaries, in which a man who has a "husband" became the top candidate in the first district. He was campaigning with his husband, and I felt odd to see it. I certainly admit that people have various sexualities, but frankly speaking, it is questionable whether this tendency should be openly accepted for a presidential candidate.

Iran condemns this tendency and probably sees this as the ultimate state of corruption. To prevent this from happening in their country, they strictly separate men and women and prohibit women from showing their faces in public. For example, a female singer is allowed to sing without covering her face in front of an all-female audience, but she must hide it when there are men because it can arouse desire in men. This custom has been traditionally taught, and the people believe it is right. They believe men and women can be drawn to each other and get married only when there is an appropriate distance between them. If everything is allowed, many people will start to go astray and society will become corrupt. They may raise such opinions and refutations.

In a different news story on the same day, I read an article related to Islam. It talked about a circumcision practice that took place in Egypt. Apparently, female circumcision practices exist in Islamic culture, and a 12-year-old girl was taken to a hospital to be circumcised but died from excessive bleeding. The parents who took her to the hospital were then arrested and charged with murder.

Islam is based on the Quran, which is a compilation of the words of God, and Hadith, a collection of sayings and deeds of Muhammad. In Hadith, there are descriptions about circumcisions for females as well as for males. This practice did not purely start with Islam but dates back thousands of years, when the practice was sought in Africa. It started there as a ceremony to make chastity compulsory, and it later spread to the desert regions. It was most probably practiced in Judaism as well, even before it was incorporated into Islamic culture. There are many women's rights groups protesting this as a violation of human rights. Since a mortality incident occurred, this issue was covered in the news. Such problems exist in Islam.

On the other hand, Christianity has become too lax, and anything is starting to be allowed. It is obvious that a clash of values would occur on this issue, so I have to somehow settle this issue. We can see that there are problems concerning sexualities.

Regarding Buddhism, the precepts set by Shakyamuni Buddha show that homosexuality, as well as what is now called bisexuality, was forbidden for renunciant disciples. Those who were described as neuter gender were also not allowed to renounce the world to become monks either, though I am not really sure if such types of people truly existed. I do not know whether this applied to laypeople as well, but because monks and nuns separately underwent spiritual training, I think these rules were set to prevent any confusion from arising.

In addition, monks and nuns were not allowed to lead a married life. Even those who were once husband and wife could not freely meet once they became monks and nuns because they basically lived in separate places. Whether these rules should be condemned or accepted is a subtle issue, but they had these rigid rules to continue living peacefully as a group. The same could be said about boarding schools; it is not possible to run a school well unless the male and female dormitories are separated, though how strictly the rules should be enforced is up for debate.

Buddhism is considered to be a rather conservative religion, but since they very strictly forbade the desires for the opposite sex, homosexual tendencies started to emerge. The same could be said of Christianity, as seen in numerous scandals involving the Vatican today. We cannot be completely exempt from sexual matters; given that men and women were created differently, it was perhaps anticipated from the very beginning that such issues would arise to some extent.

Make efforts to defend your weak points

As I mentioned earlier, if a man who underwent spiritual discipline and attained enlightenment receives pure and supportive thoughts from a woman while he carries out his activities, he is protected and can firmly stand against devils and evil spirits. This is the reason why there are many shrine maidens.

What happens when a man fights the devil while receiving support from young, pure-hearted shrine maidens? A form of pure love and faith in God are emitted from these shrine maidens, which work to support and protect the man to some extent. But if their relationship becomes calculating and impure, these will no longer serve to protect him but rather drag him down.

During the early days of Buddhism, the renunciant disciples were not allowed to marry, and it was common for them to not have any children. But after the Middle Ages in Japan, it became common for them to get married and have children. It is certainly true that having a family is a burden. For those who were devoting themselves to spiritual discipline, financial burden was probably one of their biggest concerns.

In addition, Buddha's order in the early stages was not strong enough to allow the renunciant disciples to live like normal salaried workers who work only during business hours and use the remaining time for family. If this were allowed, their lifestyle would be no different from that of laypeople; under this lifestyle, the renunciant disciples would only consume the donations from laypeople. So even if making offerings was a traditional practice, people probably could not accept such a system.

Traditionally, unmarried renunciant disciples underwent spiritual training and lived off of alms, but there was also competition with other religious groups. Oftentimes, more offerings were made to virtuous religions with respectable followers and disciples. In a way, the reputation of practicing strict discipline or having higher virtue helped gather more offerings. So even though there were no tabloids at the time, rumors and people's evaluation affected the amount of offerings received.

Even when conducting exorcisms today, devils target any potential weaknesses that exorcists may have, regardless of whether they are single or married. So the only thing you can do is defend these weak points as much as possible. Just as there are spears to attack and shields to defend, you need to defend yourself as well as attack. As I often teach, the common weaknesses that devils aim to attack are greed, anger, foolishness, pride, doubt, and false views. So it is important to block these weaknesses and make efforts to fill in any unguarded gaps you may have.

5

The Spiritual Power of the Real Exorcist

Maintaining and strengthening spiritual power by controlling yourself

Prior to this lecture, I received a question about how to assess one's progress in spiritual training, but objectively assessing this is quite difficult. Happy Science conducts the "Spiritual Health Checkup" exam, but the score of the exam does not necessarily reflect one's level of enlightenment. Staff members are given titles based on age, experience, and work ability, but their level of enlightenment may not necessarily correlate with their titles either. There may be people who used to be pure-hearted when they were young and single but lose that quality after becoming middle-aged. There are countless causes of downfall, similar to those you see in society in general.

So the simplest way to see one's spiritual progress is this: "We are preconditioned to live in this world as humans and naturally have worldly desires, so the question is how well we are able to control and restrain these earthly desires." This is often mentioned in Buddhist scriptures as well. In general, people with great achievements are often respected, but based on the teachings in the Buddhist scriptures, people are often praised for how well they have trained and controlled their minds and bodies in their daily lives, rather than for what they have accomplished in this world. What matters is the day-to-day efforts.

As you continue to accumulate such efforts, you may gradually gain recognition from the people around you. Lay believers can somehow perceive whether the prayers and exorcisms conducted by a particular priest are effective or not. So it is worth noting that one's spiritual progress is not determined by his or her job title, age, or income, as it is in regular organizations consisting of laypeople. In other words, those who make an effort to control and govern themselves will be able to maintain and strengthen their spiritual power.

Even a person who is usually peaceful can exert a strong force

As long as we live on earth, we need some desires to survive. But those who have managed to control their desires well and preserved and accumulated that energy as "savings" can more easily exert spiritual powers.

There are various forces, as demonstrated in boxing punches, kick-boxing kicks, and judo throws, but apart from these physical forces, there is a spiritual force. And those who usually live with a flexible, generous, and peaceful mind can exert a surprisingly strong force—the force of willpower. These people are usually very generous and treat many people with compassion, but at critical times, when they have to fight and defeat evil beings, they can focus their spiritual energy and drive them away. I teach various kinds of rites to dispel these evil beings, so it is better to master them if you can.

Body parts that emit spiritual power

Now, where on the body is spiritual power emitted from?

One location is the palm. Light and spiritual power emanate from the center of the palm, so hands are often used in exorcisms. Another source is between the eyebrows. It is said that there is a chakra on the forehead between the eyebrows, and indeed, strong power can be released from there. Eyes also have power in and of themselves.

The mouth is another source. Because words are produced from the mouth, you can utter words to fight against evil spirits and devils. Those with spiritual sight can see balls of Light that resemble soap bubbles coming out of the mouth when reciting "The True Words Spoken By Buddha" or other sutras and prayers of Happy Science. Because words with spiritual energy are uttered from the mouth, the words carry power. This power reflects one's overall ability. The overall ability gained from one's studies and efforts will be exerted, and this will enable you to admonish others or change their minds through your words.

Of course, the heart emits power, too. A certain amount of power of love is emitted from the area around the heart. With this power of love, you can dispel evil at times, forgive evil at other times, and melt away evil on other occasions. This kind of loving heart exists. For example, some people give off an air that discourages others from fighting them. Even people who normally commit evil deeds will not be able to do anything bad to those with overwhelming goodwill. Gangsters often target those who are off guard, and they seem to sense that certain types of people should not be targeted. So it is important to give off goodwill.

There is also a powerful spiritual field around the solar plexus in the lower abdomen. Unless you have unwavering strength around this area, it is difficult to ultimately triumph over the devil. This power goes beyond the victory or defeat measured by the logic of this world; it is far stronger than that. To exert such power, you need to have a strong will that wells up from the depth of your soul; you must have the will to save all humankind, to make this world a better place, or to prevent evil from prevailing on earth. Whether you have such a strong, indomitable determination makes a big difference.

Body movements or poses to exorcise evil spirits

Various body movements are involved in exorcisms. There are no fixed hand signs like in the art of Ninja, but the spirits that come to provide spiritual guidance will help you make the appropriate body movements or strike an appropriate pose at the time of the exorcism. So all you need to do is follow their instructions.

This is true for me as well. Some rites of exorcism, such as "El Cantare Fight," have a fixed sequence of movements to perform. Otherwise, when I need to exert or send out spiritual power, in most cases, the guiding spirit that is present at the time will have me strike its favorite pose.

If you can focus your willpower to create force, it is possible to emit Light, like a laser beam emitted from a laser gun. Different hand signs can be used to emit such Light, but you do not need to give it too much thought because you will naturally be able to strike the right pose if a proper spirit is there to guide you.

In general, the power emanated from the palm is easy to use. This power is quite effective for exorcising evil spirits. There are also poses to focus Light at a specific point. A common way to do this is by creating the form of a sword using both of your hands.

6

How to Create a Spiritual Screen against Strong Evil Spirits and Devils

The ineffectiveness of the traditional Shinto method to ward off evil

Another question I received was on how to create a spiritual screen against strong evil spirits and devils. It is very difficult to do this. In practice, Japanese Shinto, for example, uses salt to ward off evil; people place salt in the corners of the room or pile salt in the shape of a pyramid. They even believe that certain brands of salt are more effective than others. I actually tried these practices in various ways, but they were essentially a "free pass" for the spirits. The spirits paid no attention to the salt and passed right through.

There is also *shimenawa*, a sacred Shinto straw festoon. I once tried using the ones with a zigzag-shaped paper streamer (*shide*), but they did not affect the spirits either and gave them a "free pass." I am not sure if they were effective in ancient times.

Shimenawa is also used in sumo wrestling rings called *dohyo*, but I do not think the shape is what matters; I believe a spiritual field is gradually formed when many people are determined to create a sacred ring. To create a *dohyo*, ropes of rice-straw bales are embedded in a circle on the earth mound, *shimenawa* ropes are hung from above, a ritual is performed to ward off evil, and salt is sprinkled to purify the ring. If there is a collective thought of all people involved that wish to carry out a clean sumo match as a divine service for the gods to watch, a spiritual field should be created.

Phenomena malicious spirits and devils can and cannot cause

There is a Japanese movie called *Kuru* (*It Comes*). In it, the leading characters fill bowls, sake cups, and other glasses with water to fend off a mysterious evil spirit that comes from the mountains. However, these measures are not effective at all in reality. The windows, walls, or roofs are not helpful either because spirits can pass through any material.

On the other hand, spirits cannot do things such as cut people's heads off with a saw, as depicted in the movie. Things like this normally do not happen in reality. People may have sleep paralysis or faint from a sudden feeling of heaviness, but I have not met a devil that can make powerful physical phenomena happen. Although they can make certain fear-inciting physical phenomena happen to let people know of their presence or to frighten them, they generally do not have the ability to tear human flesh or to cut bodies in half. Furthermore, I am afraid I cannot accept the ideas of corpses buried in the cemetery coming back to life as zombies and killing people or of such zombies being killed by shooting them with a rifle. Presumably, various folktales and superstitions have been mixed up in such ideas.

Evil spirits and devils do truly affect electrical appliances. I am not exactly sure how this works, but there are cases where lights suddenly turn off.

People can also fall ill due to spiritual possession. If a person is possessed by bad spirits that still retain their diseased condition at the time of death, he or she can suffer a similar condition. For example, these spirits can sometimes find a way to possess someone they have a close connection to, such as a friend, parent, sibling, or relative. When this happens, the possessed person can contract the same illness as the deceased.

There are actually families in which family members contract the same illness generation after generation. If people in three consecutive generations die in the same way by contracting cancer or hanging themselves, for instance, it is usually due to spiritual possession. In this case, it is important to realize that some spiritual beings are lingering around. In other cases, certain spirits possess people from a specific family for generations, much like the Grim Reaper.

Visit Happy Science local branches and shoja regularly

There can be such spirits among one's ancestors who have been unable to return to heaven. In this case, it would be difficult to deal with them on your own, so I recommend that you attend seminars at Happy Science local branches or shoja or ask the priest to perform an exorcism.

Of course, these beings will not immediately vanish after one attempt. Most people spend the majority of their time outside holy places, so it is not easy to remove them right away. Nevertheless, it is important to find an opportunity to walk the road to enlightenment and be determined to make an effort to live differently than how these spirits had lived.

In fact, the best solution is to be like water and oil; if your mind is completely different from the minds of the spirits trying to cause harm, you will be able to repel them like oil repels water. So try to avoid having similar mindsets and fill your mind with different ways of thinking. My books and lectures will help you achieve that. In this sense, it is very important to regularly attend and listen to my lectures when they are held, participate in our seminars, and find an opportunity to talk with our priests.

We also hold rituals to exorcise evil spirits. Sometimes the spirits can be expelled after just one attempt, but if the spirits have been possessing a person for a long time, they will most likely come back to the person after they have been expelled. Therefore, it is essential to visit a shoja or local branch regularly or on a monthly basis, listen to the lectures, have an exorcism performed, and participate in other activities. Such spirits cannot be easily expelled.

Those who are able to channel spirits must humbly seek a pure mind

In the early days of Happy Science, I once made someone without enough spiritual training become capable of channeling spirits. It started out fine when his guardian spirit was visiting, but in less than a month, he started to be possessed by evil spirits. He could not expel the spirits on his own because he did not learn to channel spirits with his own ability.

In this kind of situation, it is important to return to the basics. You should get rid of the desire for fame or vanity and abandon the thoughts of whether or not you are important in this world. You should also humbly seek a pure mind and go back to carrying out spiritual discipline just as any another believer or disciple. As you continue these efforts, you will gradually return to a normal state.

As I said earlier, if black ink is added into a bucket of water one drop at a time, the water will gradually turn completely black. Conversely, if you add clean, pure water into a bucket of sullied water one drop at a time, the water will gradually overflow and become clear again. It will eventually become clean enough to be used for drinking or washing. The same can be said about spiritual matters. If you have become impure and attract beings with similar mindsets to yours, you must take in the opposite qualities—the holy elements—little by little. It is important to gradually remove the impure parts of yourself, as if peeling away thin fabric one layer at a time.

Spiritual discipline must be carried out over many years. The duration of time is important in spiritual discipline. As you keep training for a number of years, you will come across many different instances. If you continue training for 10 years, you will most likely face all kinds of situations. So those who have been lecturers for 20 or 30 years at Happy Science have gained a certain amount of strength. In many cases, they have power.

However, when they attain a higher status after many years of spiritual discipline, they may become conceited and start neglecting their discipline a little. When this happens, they will become unable to exorcise evil spirits and instead become the target of the attack. So it is important for disciples to watch out for one another.

Be connected to El Cantare and you will be protected

There are people who dislike being involved in religious organizations. They may think it is enough to just buy Happy Science books at the bookstore and read them alone or to simply attend my open lectures independently. There have always been many people who dislike restrictions or rules placed by organizations.

These people have the tendency of a self-styled practitioner, but they need to know that by training within the organization, they can be protected by the collective power of believers. One is weak when fighting on an individual level. But when many people belonging to a large organization carry out the same kind of spiritual training and have similar mindsets, their collective thought works like an embankment to prevent any flooding.

By training yourself within that environment, you can ultimately be connected to El Cantare and to El Cantare's supporting spirit group. Being connected to such a grand network will work as the power to protect yourself. If you are connected to the entire network, no devil can stand a chance to win. It is important to realize that there is a limit to how much one can fight on the individual level.

This concludes my talk on the condition of the real exorcist. I hope it will be of some help to you.

CHAPTER FOUR

The Right Way to Conquer the Devils

Spiritual Power to Make the World Brighter

Originally recorded in Japanese on October 4, 2020,
at Holy Land El Cantare Seitankan of Happy Science, Tokushima Prefecture in Japan,
and later translated into English.

1

Religious Enlightenment to Dispel Viruses, Malicious Spirits, and Devils

Overcoming problems no matter what may happen

We held only a few public lectures in 2020, so our members may not have felt very satisfied. After giving a public lecture in Kan'onji City, Kagawa Prefecture in February and another lecture in Sendai City, Miyagi Prefecture in March, some critical articles came out saying that Happy Science was nonchalantly holding lectures in front of over 1,000 people. I was a little surprised to find that people in general were so nervous and were holding back their activities. But I thought it was best not to provoke them too much and decided to release my recorded lectures for people to watch at smaller venues instead for the time being.

We had plans to go to London in May to give a public lecture, but due to the spread of the novel coronavirus, gatherings of three or more people were banned in London at the time. Later, the restrictions were relieved to gatherings of seven or more people, but we could not hold a lecture under those circumstances. So we unfortunately had to forgo the plan. We also had plans to give a lecture in New York in September, but New York was another "hard-fought field"; it was actually the location that was hit the hardest by the coronavirus outbreak. So we had to give that up as well. There are times when things do not go according to plan.

Many things have happened since I started this work a long time ago, but no matter what happened, I devised new ways to overcome obstacles every time. Because this time was no exception, I decided to focus on what needs to be internally done and on storing preparations as "savings" so that I can start giving lectures when the time comes for us to freely hold lectures at various places.

This past summer, I worked hard on writing the original stories for the movies that will come out in a few years because we all had to stay at home. You may be able to watch them when you have "aged" a little more. Anyway, it is good for me to write stories for movies early while my sensibilities are still sharp.

No one in the audience at Happy Science lectures has contracted the coronavirus

This chapter, "The Right Way to Conquer the Devils," is a lecture that was given in October 2020 at Holy Land El Cantare Seitankan of Happy Science in Tokushima Prefecture on Shikoku Island. But my original plan was to give this lecture there much earlier to kick-start our movie *The Real Exorcist* (Executive Producer and original story by Ryuho Okawa), which was scheduled to be released in May. However, at the time, some cars with out-of-prefecture license plates parked there were being reported to the police. This normally does not happen, and I do not think there should be any problem with cars coming from neighboring prefectures, but because it was such a tense time, we decided to forgo the lecture.

However, so far, not a single person has contracted the coronavirus from attending my lecture. So there is nothing to be worried about. There were certainly cases where religious gatherings were considered dangerous after some believers of other religious groups contracted the coronavirus at churches, but that is because they have a slightly different faith. The coronavirus spread widely in South Korea as well, and one of the Christian churches, which is said to be a heretical group, saw hundreds of their followers contracting the virus after a gathering. But this does not happen at Happy Science.

At the end of August 2020, Happy Science released a documentary movie called *Living in the Age of Miracles* (original concept by Ryuho Okawa), and from a year prior, we were searching for stories of people who had overcome serious illnesses. When the coronavirus began to spread around February and March, I suggested that we add a couple of examples of people who had recovered from the coronavirus infection in the movie. The movie crew then searched for such cases but could not find any, so we had nothing to include in the movie.

They apparently found one case: A non-member living in the U.S. was hospitalized for contracting the coronavirus and a high fever but quickly recovered from the infection after her Japanese relative and Happy Science member in Japan took a Kigan called "Prayer for Defeating the Infection of Novel Coronavirus Originated in China." But the crew considered this to be too common for it to be in a movie about miracles, so it was not included.

Happy Science members basically do not contract the coronavirus. Unfortunately, we cannot show proof of miracles with regard to the coronavirus infections, but the fact that everyone is staying healthy is a wonderful thing.

The soul of Prime Minister Johnson came to seek help

President Trump who had been working hard without a mask finally became infected by the coronavirus in October and was admitted to a hospital. At the time, I believed he would make a quick recovery and present himself in a healthy state again, and I prayed for it to be true (after this remark, President Trump was discharged from the hospital and returned to his work after being hospitalized for three days).

Perhaps contracting the virus was not all that bad for him; the accusations by the media have slightly eased, and Mr. Biden also announced that he had removed a commercial criticizing Mr. Trump. Mr. Trump is usually a little too aggressive, so it was probably good that he gained a little sympathy. I am sure that as the president of a large country, he will overcome the illness with his own strong power. I, myself, have a mission to continue doing what I must do, no matter what may happen in the world.

When Mr. Trump contracted the coronavirus, his guardian spirit did not come to me for help. On the other hand, the spirit of Prime Minister Johnson of the U.K. came to me in April, perhaps because we had plans to visit the U.K. I had never experienced anything like this before; just after I finished my dinner, I sensed what seemed to be an *ikiryo* (spirit of a living person) suddenly weighing down on me. As I was wondering who it could be, it started speaking in English and it turned out to be Mr. Johnson. At the time, Mr. Johnson was in the ICU and was about to be moved back to a regular room in the hospital, but he apparently came to ask me to pour spiritual light into him.

I think it was his soul and not his guardian spirit. His soul probably left his body to come all the way to Tokyo. After we talked for a while, he rapidly recovered and returned to work again. Mr. Trump's guardian spirit did not visit me, so I assumed his condition was not as serious, but if he did, I was intending to cure him.

Malignant viruses will leave your body if you are emitting a halo

From my perspective, the coronavirus infection is not a big problem. I usually deal with much stronger opponents, so contracting pneumonia from a coronavirus infection is a mild case that can be easily cured. So there is no need to worry. I also created music called "THE THUNDER—a composition for repelling the Coronavirus" and have released it nationally and worldwide to fight against the virus.

So why can the coronavirus infection be cured? Ultimately, if you harmonize and concentrate your mind and maintain a state of mind that allows you to slightly emit a halo—even as small as a few centimeters (about an inch)—normal malicious spirits and devils will not be able to continue possessing you. This being so, something as petty as a malignant virus will not be able to keep possessing you either.

If you can create a state of mind that allows you to emit a faint halo from your body, these viruses will leave you. This applies not only to the coronavirus but also to the flu and other infectious diseases. In the case of virus-related diseases, creating a mental state in which your entire body emanates a halo will surely help repel the viruses.

In some cases, the viruses may just move to the person next to you, so the actual number of viruses may not decrease, but at least they will move away from you. In that sense, religious enlightenment is effective for curing diseases. This is an obvious fact. This point is connected to the main points of this chapter.

2

Conquering the Devils with the Power of Enlightenment

Dispelling devils with the power of enlightenment or Dharma power

This chapter's theme, conquering the devils, is pronounced as *"gouma"* in Japanese and the Japanese *kanji* characters for it are difficult to read. But on the day I gave this lecture, I was impressed to see that the signs of the lecture title at Holy Land El Cantare Seitankan did not have a phonetic guide. Whereas people with a religion can read these *kanji* characters, those who have no knowledge of religion usually cannot, and they do not know what the expression means. Some may even misinterpret it to mean the complete opposite and understand it to mean "to summon the devils," but it would be a huge problem if a devil were to enter your body.

In fact, *gouma* means to defeat demons and devils with the power of enlightenment, or Dharma power, and to dispel them. This concept may be easier for the people of Shikoku Island to understand because Kobo Daishi Kukai (774–835), who was born and active in Shikoku Island, fought devils with his Dharma power. He had very strong Dharma power as an esoteric Buddhist monk, so I think the people in Shikoku can understand the idea better than those in other places.

Around May 2021, we plan to release a movie related to this theme after *Twiceborn* (Executive Producer and original story by Ryuho Okawa), which came out in theaters in October 2020. The new movie is about a reincarnation of Kukai confronting the modern *youma* (foxy witch, or foxy demon) and is titled *Beautiful Lure—A Modern Tale of "Painted Skin"* (Executive Producer and original story by Ryuho Okawa). The filming process is already complete, and we are now adding some computer graphics. So you will be able to see another exorcism-related movie.

Lately, we have been extensively researching on the rear side of the spirit world and introducing various beings residing there. They have different tendencies, so if you know them and can quickly recognize the specific cases, it is easier to mentally prepare yourself.

Lecturing in India about conquering the devils

The origins of the expression "conquering the devils" generally go back to Gautama Siddhartha, who was born in Nepal and was active in India 2,500–2,600 years ago. After leaving Kapilavastu and undergoing ascetic training in the fields and mountains for six years, he fought an army of devils while meditating under a large Bodhi tree. The devils challenged him, as if they were in a final, decisive battle, but he defeated them with his power of meditation. This battle is depicted in old films as well as in some of Happy Science's animated movies.

The Bodhi tree under which Gautama Siddhartha attained enlightenment stands in the precincts of Mahabodhi Temple, which I visited when I went to India on a missionary tour. The large tree growing there now is the grandchild or the great-grandchild of the original tree under which Shakyamuni Buddha meditated. There is a big open space in front of the big temple, and I gave an English lecture there to an audience of over 40,000 people (the lecture "The Real Buddha and New Hope" was held on March 6, 2011).

Because it was a vast open space, it took over one month for the carpenters to build pillars and set up a tent-like structure as a venue for my lecture. The venue was built to fit an audience of 40,000 people and was partitioned off with large pieces of cloth. But on the day of my lecture, the space overflowed with people who came on foot from various places. More and more people kept arriving, which made me worry whether I could start my talk on time.

As I walked toward the podium, I saw the highest-ranking monks of the Mahabodhi Temple sitting in the front. The first few rows were filled by the authentic monks of India—the Buddhist homeland. I felt a little stumped because I had intended to talk about simple topics for the general public. But because the top monks were all staring at me, hoping to hear about what enlightenment is, I changed my mind and decided to talk about "the Middle Way" and "conquering the devils and attaining enlightenment," even though these topics may have been a little difficult.

I am not sure if the rest of the 40,000 people were able to comprehend my lecture, but because it was broadcasted on national TV multiple times, some people may have been able to understand my lecture after watching it a few times. It was nationally broadcasted on national TV in Nepal as well. Unlike the Japanese, other people are quite enthusiastic about religious teachings. They are very supportive of religious activities, and I hope Japanese people will be able to sense the difference in people's attitude toward religion.

Happy Science is slowly gaining recognition across the world

We are still fortunate compared with other religious groups in Japan. The two lectures we hold annually on the occasions of the "Celebration of the Lord's Descent" in the summer and "El Cantare Celebration" in the winter are now broadcasted through five or six regional TV stations. TV Wakayama and some other channels broadcast them every year, and people in the neighboring prefectures can view these lectures. These media companies have agreed to broadcast my lectures but not those of other religions, so I believe they have accepted Happy Science to some extent.

On the contrary, the key stations that broadcast programs across Japan will not air my lectures unless I get involved in an incident that causes a stir in society. They will definitely do so when I die, but while I am still alive, they will not allow my lectures to be aired so easily and try hard to resist. Even so, we are slowly gaining recognition in various ways.

The coronavirus is now widely spreading across the globe, but Happy Science is also fighting a different kind of battle around the world. According to the internal report I received in August 2021, there are Happy Science members in 164 countries, so perhaps we have expanded even further now. If everyone gets well just from listening to the music I produce, such as "THE THUNDER—a composition for repelling the Coronavirus" or "THE EXORCISM—prayer music for repelling Lost Spirits," this would be a very effective way of fighting in modern times.

The aforementioned movie *The Real Exorcist* received over 50 awards overseas, which was very surprising even for us. We received so many awards from all categories that I cannot remember them all. I think this is because other countries are more receptive to religious matters.

This movie is on exorcisms, but we simply gathered episodes of what we considered to be "ordinary" to put in the movie. We certainly made the final battle more exciting to watch, but otherwise, the movie contained ordinary episodes that commonly happen in life. This apparently seemed to be an unusual approach for people who make many exorcism or horror-related movies; they probably thought, "What? Is that it? Shouldn't it be more dreadful and frightening so that the characters are running around in fear?" Our movie dealt with cases that commonly happen in life, and this seemed to have given them a unique impression. I am truly grateful that people can appreciate our movie. I feel there is still hope in the world.

3

Conquering the Devils Depicted in the Movie *Twiceborn*

Twiceborn *clearly portrays the fight to conquer the devils*

Shakyamuni Buddha's Great Enlightenment is often referred to as "conquering the devils and attaining enlightenment." It means he defeated the devils and completed his way to the Truth. This certainly was not the final goal, but it means he attained the first great enlightenment.

The Buddhist scriptures describe how the Buddha conquered the devils in many different ways, but in general, it is said that an army of devils consisting of the first, second, and third unit appeared on elephants in succession and surrounded the Buddha as they attacked him with various weapons. The Buddha defeated these devils in a calm state of meditation, and this act of conquering the devils led to his attainment of enlightenment under the Bodhi tree. That is why it is said that "conquering the devils is attaining enlightenment."

In fact, by attaining enlightenment, one is granted Dharma power—the spiritual power to dispel devils. Many Buddhist scholars today say that this battle refers to the internal conflicts and concerns in the Buddha's mind, but this is not true. As I have explained in many books, this battle is not simply an internal conflict but an actual experience of fighting the devils. It is real and something that actually happened.

You can see a glimpse of this fight once again in the movie *Twiceborn*, which was released on October 16, 2020. The movie depicts the path I took to my attainment of enlightenment up to the day I gave my first grand lecture at Tokyo Dome; the movie shows what it truly was like.

The final battle to conquer the devils always happens right before the attainment of enlightenment. A movie we made two years ago also had a similar scene portraying how I fought this battle, but it failed to clearly describe what I truly went through to conquer the devils. This battle is very important; one cannot call oneself "truly enlightened" unless he or she has conquered the devils. That is why we carefully gathered various materials to restructure the story and recreated the movie, which turned out to be a completely different film.

The devils' fierce attack just before attaining enlightenment

The movie *Twiceborn* is quite the masterpiece. It won over 20 international awards even before it was released in Japan, which showed how promising it is. It is indeed a great piece and is longer than most movies.

To tell the truth, the movie director suggested that we make it shorter by cutting 16 minutes. But I asked him not to do so because I did not see any scenes that could be omitted. I did not think we would have another chance to make a movie on the same theme, and it would also be difficult for me to recall the memories of my youth again, so I had this kind of negotiation with the director on whether or not to make the movie 16 minutes shorter.

I asked him, "Please don't cut any part of it. We've already filmed it and cannot shoot it again, so let's leave it as is. This movie is based on facts, and it depicts all that actually happened, so nothing needs to be omitted." I even left him a note saying, "The executive producer is asking not to shorten the film. Isn't this a great honor for the director?" I finally convinced him by saying, "Usually, executive directors ask for the opposite to be done, so it should be an honor for a director to be asked not to cut any part of the film; it means there is no part to be omitted."

Movie theaters do not like it when movies are longer than 120 minutes. Because they care about the number of showings per day, they want to avoid movies that are over two hours. Our movie was about 10 minutes longer. But because other big movies that became a huge international hit are usually 140–150 minutes long and do not end in two hours either, we decided to keep the movie as it was; it was already a masterpiece.

One of the highlights toward the end of the movie is the scene in which the main character conquers the devils and attains enlightenment. In this movie, we tried our best to stay true to what I experienced and reproduced the real events using computer graphics. You can study the theme of this chapter once again by watching the movie.

Let me explain a little further about what had happened to me. Usually, spiritual possession by evil spirits and devils can occur when your mind is in a bad condition, but there are also other cases that do not follow this pattern. In the case of religious practitioners, the devils make a final, fierce attack on them just before they attain enlightenment. This has happened throughout history; it happened to Shakyamuni Buddha as well as to Jesus.

In the face of their overwhelming strength and power, I understood how desperate these devils were in trying to prevent me from leaving my job at the company and starting Happy Science. I realized that fulfilling my mission would put them in real trouble; they simply wanted me to give up so that I would leave them alone and let them keep their evil empire safe.

Now that more than 70 years have passed since World War II, the devils have succeeded in manipulating the Japanese education system to make people uncertain about the existence of the other world. Medical science has advanced further but only with a focus on materialistic science. Doctors try to cure illnesses just by conducting surgeries to cut and remove parts of the body, such as internal organs, or by prescribing medicines. Materialistic thinking is prevailing in this way, which is a huge problem.

The spiritual reason behind people's violent rejections of the Truth

In the past, I experienced the following issue. I went to see a doctor, and he apparently read a Happy Science book that was given to him before our appointment. Until then, I had not had any issues with that doctor, who was a gentle person, but on that particular day, he seemed gloomy and appeared to be under a negative spiritual influence. He read how illnesses can be cured through miracles, but this notion seemed to have been quite a shock to his soul; it may have felt like being struck in the head with a metal bat. To my surprise, he was possessed by a devil.

Normally, he is not the kind of person who would be possessed by a devil, so it means that the notion of illnesses being cured through miracles was a blow to medical science as well. Doctors do not learn about it or actually experience it themselves, so it was perhaps unacceptable to him. He was totally bewildered, which was quite a surprise to me.

Truth is this powerful, and it can stimulate others in an unexpected way. You may have also experienced various negative reactions when giving books of Truth to others or telling people about the Truth. However, please be strong.

People who accept books of Truth without hesitation and say, "Oh, this is a good book," are like lotus flowers that are about to bloom and can easily understand the Truth. But normally, people will reject or resist your offer. One of the reasons for this is that they will no longer be able to live in the comfortable way they used to live if they accept the value system of the Truth. Another reason is because of the various spirits possessing them. Among the spirits of their ancestors, family members, friends, co-workers, those suffering from illnesses, or those who died in accidents, some may have fallen to hell and become evil spirits after death. If people are possessed by such spirits, they will reject the Truth even more intensely because the possessing spirits loathe it.

On the day I gave this lecture, too, there may well have been some phenomena occurring at the main venue or the satellite venues. Some people may have been swaying side to side or back and forth, whereas others may have fallen asleep. In other cases, some people may have even fallen over sideways, backward, or forward in their chairs or have found their bodies stiffening and collapsed. There are also cases where people foam at the mouth or blow snot bubbles. These phenomena are all spiritual reactions. Those who witness these might be surprised, but there is no need to worry. They are the signs that the possessing spirits are starting to leave. So if you feel that something is possessing you, I hope you will take this opportunity to start studying the Truth.

The reason why I continue to speak about the spiritual Truth

There are many people who cannot believe in spiritual matters even if they read or hear about them. When you tell them the Truth, they may say, "It's just a delusion of one's mind," "It's an old tale," or "Don't talk about such spooky stories during the day when I'm working." People usually separate spiritual matters from their actual lives, so in many cases, they cannot understand the Truth you are trying to convey.

Happy Science broadcasts a radio program called "Angel's Morning Call" in the morning every weekend on 36 radio stations across Japan and one station overseas, and the number of stations broadcasting it is increasing. In addition to talks by a personality, the program introduces excerpts from my lectures and the music I wrote and composed.

When this radio program was recently launched at one of the local radio stations in Japan, the CEO of the station was also there to listen. The main topic of that day was "guardian spirits," so the personality started the talk by saying, "Good morning, everyone. Today, I would like to talk about guardian spirits." Upon hearing this, the CEO apparently got worried and suggested, "Why not start the program with a more ordinary topic? Talking about guardian spirits in the morning on a weekend may be a little too spooky."

We did not have such concerns perhaps because our senses have become numb from dealing with such topics for many years. Although we see these topics as a matter of course, they are not ordinary topics for those who are not interested in the spiritual world.

We also publish a significant number of books on spiritual messages. Some people say there is no need to publish so many books, but by presenting the different thoughts and characters of the spirits, we are trying to inform people that various spirits exist. I truly want people to know that we are spiritual beings and will return to the other world after we die. Even when we are alive, we all have a guardian spirit—one of our soul siblings— who tries to help us and give us advice. As we live, we are affected by different kinds of spiritual influences from other people as well. I want people to know that this is the kind of world we live in.

4

Secrets of the Universe That Lie beyond Science on Earth

Happy Science is providing information through UFO Reading and Space People Reading

In addition to publishing books on spiritual messages, we have started to publish books regarding UFO Reading and Space People Reading in recent years. Some people may worry about what I am doing, but when I have come this far, there is no point in stopping. I have to reveal everything I should because I will run out of time if I hesitate. So I have decided to publish what must be published. Japan was lagging behind in the field of UFO research, but it is now catching up and joining the advanced nations after Happy Science started to release various kinds of information on this topic.

In the spring of 2020, the Trump administration released three video footages of unidentified flying objects, or UFOs, that supposedly carried extraterrestrial beings. There should be a far greater number of records of UFO sightings in reality; nevertheless, the U.S. government has finally made an official announcement of the existence of these beings. In Japan, on the other hand, the Minister of Defense at the time said something along the lines of, "I myself do not believe in UFOs, but now that the U.S. has officially approved of them, we have asked the Self-Defense Forces, especially the Air Self-Defense Forces, to collect as much evidence as possible by taking photos of them, for example."

Happy Science is also trying hard to present reference materials on this topic. It is impossible for life forms to exist only on Earth in this vast universe. There are trillions of galaxies that have star systems and countless planets that have similar environments to ours. There are many planets that satisfy the conditions under which life forms can be born. Furthermore, we cannot necessarily say that all planets are experiencing the same stages of development at the same time; there should be planets that are more advanced and others that are still developing. Because life forms exist on Earth, it is likely that those from other advanced planets are here to observe us.

Not all materialists disagree on this topic. Some say that they cannot completely deny the possibility of other humanoids existing in other parts of the universe; they think this could be possible according to the laws of evolution and if the environment permits it. To prove this, we need to explain how these life forms travel such a long distance, but the current level of science on Earth is not advanced enough to do so.

My talk about UFOs and the universe will spread to many countries in the world

Humans may finally be able to land on Mars during our grandchildren's generation if one can afford to pay ¥200 million (about US$2 million). But it may not be as exciting as one would think because there is not much to see on Mars. One may be able to bring back a piece of rock at best.

Humans may also be able to travel to the moon one day, but because there are many things that "should not be witnessed" on the other side of the moon, there are still hurdles to overcome. When the U.S. conducted the Apollo project, they saw and recorded many things they should not have witnessed on the other side of the moon. Since then, they became scared and stopped going to the moon. But I think people will eventually start to visit the moon again.

People naturally feel fear when they see something unknown. But once they hear the explanations on what those "secrets" are, they will likely be able to gain a general understanding of them.

Among our souls, there are those that inhabit planets other than Earth. When they complete their soul training on that planet, they can migrate to Earth and undergo soul training again. There are also those that graduate from Earth to move on to another planet. I also teach that the realm of high spirits in the highest dimension of the spirit world, which we call the "Cosmic Realm," is connected to other planets.

From a worldly perspective, it might be better not to talk about this topic, but if I do not, who else can tell the Truth? Even if my disciples say the same thing, they may not be taken seriously, so I am determined to say all that I have to say. If I talk about how UFOs and space people have been visiting Earth, this information will spread to over 160 countries because Happy Science has believers in 164 countries. This is a favorable situation for the space people, and that is why they sometimes send us revelations from space.

Having said this, I publish books on not only spiritual messages and space-related topics but also general themes, such as the ways of thinking based on religious thought or ideal ways to live as a human. I talk about space-related matters only on the premise that the fundamental principle—living life in the right way as human beings—is preserved. While maintaining this point, I also try to expand and dig deeper into other fields that people may have an interest in or want to know more about.

How the magnetic field of Earth's spirit world is formed

It seems like scientists have yet to succeed in exploring the spirit world. The Earth orbits around the Sun while rotating on its axis, and based on what I see, a magnetic field is formed as the Earth rotates over 24 hours. This magnetic field is split into several layers. It appears to me that a multi-dimensional spirit world is formed in the magnetic field that is created by the rotation of the Earth.

The layer closest to the Earth's surface is the realm called the "fourth dimension," followed by the fifth dimension above it, then the sixth dimension and so on. In this way, the spirit world is formed in layers as the Earth rotates. I presume there are also such magnetic fields on other planets where humanoid life forms exist.

5

The Essence of Conquering the Devils

The simple Truth that greatly changes your life

Although science is still unable to explain the spirit world, the Truth lies in what the Buddha said 2,500–2,600 years ago. In fact, the other world, or the Real World, is the true world, and part of our souls occasionally reincarnates on earth. Although this is quite a simple idea, your life can greatly change depending on whether or not you can accept it.

The invisible other world is our true home, and we are occasionally born into this world to gain new experiences because this world undergoes changes of eras. This world is the only place where souls of different levels gather, and herein lies the meaning of being born into this world. Just like potatoes are peeled as they rub against each other, we polish each other as we go to various schools, work in companies, or do work in an environment where there is no telling of who is a great soul and who is not. In this sense, this world on earth is meaningful.

In the other world, our souls inhabit different dimensions depending on the level of our souls, but when we are reborn on earth, we gather in the same place. As we undergo soul training in this world, some will make mistakes and end up in hell, where they will carry out spiritual training for several hundred years. Once they have completed their self-reflection, they will ascend to a slightly higher level in the spirit world and be given another chance to be reborn on earth. We teach this simple view of the world. We always reach this conclusion no matter how many times we conduct various research on it, so it is better for everyone to accept this view.

The meaning of "freedom" taught at Happy Science

Because both Happy Science and the Happiness Realization Party advocate the values of "Freedom, Democracy, and Faith," some people may argue that they should be free to do anything they want because it is their lives in this world. However, I have to say, "Wait a minute."

If people believed they should do whatever they want because life is limited to this world and they will die in several years or decades, then some might decide to climb onto a platform with a machine gun and kill hundreds of people, like in extreme movies. However, that would not be the end of their story. Even a death sentence is not the end. They will have to repent for a long period of time after that. That is why one should not do such things.

Freedom comes with responsibility, so in case you do something wrong, there is always a negative consequence.

Therefore, make it your ideal to bring happiness to other people by freely doing what you think is right.

The world will appear to be beautiful and shining when you become spiritually awakened

Some people may think that they can only be happy when they get something or when certain conditions are fulfilled. However, when you become more spiritually awakened, the world will truly appear to be beautiful and shining. This is described in the lyrics of the song, "From Sadness to Delight" (written and composed by Ryuho Okawa, the feature song of the movie *Living in the Age of Miracles*).

Different kinds of people are making efforts to attain their own enlightenment as they live in various family and work environments. If you can feel that the world is beautiful when looking at these people and leave this world with such a feeling, then you can say your life was a success.

When I saw everyone who gathered to listen to this lecture, I felt that the world is beautiful. To my eyes, everyone sitting in the audience was shining like pure gold, though they may have been slightly "coated" with something else.

As I often teach, one of the characteristics of those who go to hell is the tendency to blame others or the environment when something inconvenient or unhappy occurs to them. This is their biggest mistake. Everyone who went to hell has such a trait. To put it bluntly, they are self-centered. Self-centered people who have gone to hell are told to reflect on their words and deeds, are secluded, or are bullied by ogres. Hell is such a place.

On the contrary, those who tried to benefit others by working for others, making people happy, or working to make the world more beautiful have all returned to heaven. The truth is as simple as this.

So if you self-centeredly keep blaming other people or the environment and keep thinking you have become unhappy because of this or that, you are on the wrong track. You have to change your ways of thinking. You are given many things. You are blessed with many things, too. It is a wonderful thing.

On the day I gave this lecture, my former classmate and my math teacher at Kawashima Junior High School also came to the main venue. After graduating from Kawashima Junior High School, I eventually went to the University of Tokyo, competed among the brilliant students from the elite schools in Tokyo and Osaka, and never lost to them. This shows that the education at Kawashima Junior High School and Jonan High School of Tokushima Prefecture, which I attended, was not at all bad. After all, it all depends on one's awareness and efforts. Everything will become wonderful if you are aware of your own mission and make efforts.

So, let us try not to make excuses by saying, "I cannot be successful because I'm from the countryside" or "I'm no good because I'm from a poor family," for example. We are all in different environments and our starting points may have been different, but we are being judged based on how far we have come from our starting points. So try to look at yourself from this perspective.

You may have had various handicaps. Some people may have lost their parents when they were born, experienced bankruptcy, or financially suffered. Others may not have been able to go to school, but even so, if they decide to study after becoming working adults, they can find many ways to do so. And if they continue their efforts, they will definitely become smart. So there are no obstacles you cannot overcome.

Since you were born, have you made the world beautiful?

When I give lectures in Tokyo, I often speak about the importance of "starting from the ordinary," but here I would like to talk about the opposite. Even if you may believe you are an ordinary person, you are not. Gold dust can be found anywhere. Wherever you are, there will always be good friends, good teachers, and good guidance. You can find such people in any company you work for.

You are mistaken if you think that good superiors can only be found in large companies and not in small ones. That is not true at all. There are many people who can serve as your "teachers of life" in various places. It is important to learn from these people and continue to refine yourself.

And be aware that the world is beautiful.

In the aforementioned song, "From Sadness to Delight," there is a verse that says, "Since I was born, how much beauty could I add to this world?" This is exactly what I am talking about.

Since you were born, have you made the world beautiful?

Did you make the world a better place?

Please ask yourself these questions. If you can answer "yes" to these questions, it means your life was a success. I hope you will live your life with this mindset.

Some people may feel overwhelmed by the various information I talked about in this lecture, but the basic idea is very simple: Find the meaning of being born into this world, live out a life of helping other people, and graduate from this world beautifully. This way of life is important. It is the mission of religion to teach this simple truth.

If people only study the academic studies of this world without learning the Truth, many will become lost spirits and wander around this world after death because they will not be able to make the final leap from this world to the other world. Furthermore, there is a world that is ruled by demons and devils. These demons and devils control such spirits, form groups that are similar to organized crime syndicates, and do many evil things by using their minions. There are such beings among those that stay in hell for a long time. Once joining such groups, it is difficult to get out of them. This is the same in this world as well as in the spirit world. Some spirits are actually trapped in such groups.

Aim for a higher sense of spirituality and become a shining star

The essence of conquering the devils is to know your brilliance based on the knowledge of the spiritual views of the world. It is also to know the brilliance of the other people around you and to live a life of gratitude and giving back. If you can live in this way, you will naturally be able to conquer the devils. So there is no need to be too afraid.

All people have at least a small amount of spiritual power, or Dharma power, and as I mentioned in the beginning, you will be able to emit a slight halo by studying the Truth. This will be possible through spiritual training. Then, various evil beings will no longer be able to possess you. This happens because of the Law of Same Wavelengths.

Although there may be a disparity among people's levels of awareness, everyone can attain a certain level of enlightenment. This is in line with the idea of democracy.

So please seek a higher sense of spirituality. Developing intelligence through academic studies will certainly serve as a basis for you to succeed and contribute to this world, but this should not be your final goal. It is very important to ultimately aim for a higher sense of spirituality.

I pray from my heart that every one of you will become a shining star. Let us do our best.

CHAPTER FIVE

Creation from Faith

Secrets to Overcoming the Crisis
Humanity Faces

Originally recorded in Japanese on July 12, 2020,
at Head Temple Sohonzan Shoshinkan of Happy Science, Tochigi Prefecture in Japan,
and later translated into English.

1

The Unexpected Adversity in the World

There is no need to be overly fearful of the coronavirus

Various adversities people would never have anticipated occurred in the year 2020. Because many large event halls were not open for use, we held this lecture for the Celebration of Lord's Descent at Sohonzan Shoshinkan (one of the Head Temples of Happy Science) and broadcasted it live to places around the world.

I, myself, like to have a large audience, so when I am told to make things smaller and smaller, I feel as if I am losing strength and shrinking, like a black hole. I cannot help feeling very sad. People overseas watched this lecture through a live broadcast, and we also arranged for the lecture to be broadcasted to the homes of people who live in areas where gatherings are not allowed. But even if people can hold gatherings, they are required to distance themselves. Seeing various restrictions placed these days, it seems like the day I can teach "The Laws of the Universe" is moving further and further away. I feel that the "laws of this world" are rather rigid and difficult.

As we continued holding lectures for an audience of a few hundred or a little over 1,000 people even after February, some media criticized us in their articles by saying, "Happy Science is gathering many people to hold events. They are quite bold." I could not understand what they meant by "bold" because I was just doing my job as usual. We were holding normal, small-scale events in the local regions, but other groups apparently could not have any gatherings at all.

I wonder what people believe in. They probably believe in the opinions of a small number of specialists in a specific area of medicine within modern science, but that is nonsense. There is no way people will get infected by the coronavirus by listening to my lecture. That is impossible.

Viruses are far from being called living organisms. If we were as big as whales, the viruses would only be the size of plankton. So there is no way they can defeat us. If you have this kind of strong will, you will definitely be safe. But those who are overwhelmed by fear and are looking for ways to get sick and die will take this as an opportunity to fall ill and become hospitalized. There are many people like this who rush to the hospital and end up getting worse and die.

People are making a great fuss over the coronavirus. The number of people who died of pneumonia caused by the coronavirus in Japan is over 15,000, and the total number of infected people is about 980,000 (as of August 5, 2021). But the total number of deaths in Japan is said to have decreased by more than 17,000 people compared with the previous year (based on the October 2020 report). In fact, the number of deaths caused by the coronavirus is very small compared with other illnesses. For example, 100–200 people out of the 14 million residents of Tokyo tested positive or had a temperature of more than 37.5°C (99.5°F) around the time I gave this lecture, but this is an extremely low rate of infection; the probability is so low that you would not even hit an infected person if you were to randomly throw a stone at a crowd.

It makes me a little sad to see people continuing to shrink and stopping all kinds of activities. They are losing against fear. Their sense of fear is taking over them and causing them to stay at home for months. I believe there is no need to be so fearful because you can easily win against the virus with the power of faith.

President Trump encouraged churches to stay open amidst the coronavirus pandemic

The coronavirus continues to spread in many countries. I think these countries do not have enough power to fight because Happy Science teachings have not spread wide enough.

In the U.S., President Trump encouraged churches to stay open even amidst the coronavirus pandemic; he said to leave them open even when gatherings were banned in other places.

I thought this was a great decision. What he meant to say is that places of worship must stay open and people should not be stopped from going there to pray to God. In his mind, he knows that faith is above medical science, which is just a field of science in modern academics. The U.S. is now trying to rise again from a very difficult situation, but I pray that the country will make a comeback and become a strong leader again.

In the U.S., over 35 million people are said to have contracted the coronavirus (as of August 5, 2021), but it is simply because Happy Science is lagging behind in its missionary work. If our teachings had spread a little further, things would not have been as bad as they are now.

The coronavirus is also spreading in Muslim countries, and gatherings have been banned in many places. Unfortunately, there is no answer from Allah there. If they called out and prayed toward the East, I could send them Light, but because they are praying upward, their prayers do not often reach me.

El Cantare: The name of God who has been watching over humankind

Throughout human history, many things have happened; many illnesses emerged, various natural disasters and catastrophes occurred, and wars took place. Many things, indeed, have happened. There were times when the population was reduced to half or a third. I have watched over different ages. I have shared in both the delight and sadness of humankind.

Now I appear before you as Ryuho Okawa. About 90 percent of Japanese people know the name, Ryuho Okawa, but if a survey were to be conducted with the question, "Have you heard of El Cantare?" the percentage of those who are familiar with the name will probably be greatly reduced. I am not sure if people know the name El Cantare. I am curious to see which is higher, the number of Happiness Realization Party supporters or the number of people who know the name El Cantare, but I have not gotten to investigating it because I feel scared to know the results. I think far fewer people know El Cantare than they do Ryuho Okawa.

Nevertheless, now is the time for people around the world who believe in God and religion to call out the name of God. It would be sad if you do not know the name of God at such a time.

Many religions were founded in the past. I am not saying that they are not helpful; many of them are effective even today. However, methods of transportation were limited and people could not travel easily during the times when those teachings were taught individually. But now the world is connected as one, which has especially become clear with the current coronavirus pandemic. The virus that originated in Wuhan, China, spread all over the world in no time. And more people have been infected on the other side of the globe than in China, where it all began. The true nature of the virus is a matter of debate, so I will not go into great detail here. But we must know that the whole world is now connected in both a good and bad way.

I currently give teachings in Japan, but these teachings will not be confined only to Japan, and Happy Science will not be confined only to Japan, either. My lectures also reach Uganda, for example, and people there gather to listen to my lectures, even in villages far from the capital. I always keep this in mind whenever I speak.

2

The Miraculous Age Is about to Begin

The miracle in Africa: A child revived from death

In the documentary movie *Living in the Age of Miracles*, released in August 2020, there is a scene where one of the main reporters visits a village in Uganda and is welcomed by the residents. He reports on a miracle that happened in central Africa, a location far away from Japan: A little girl who was considered dead from a medical perspective came back to life when her father continuously recited "The True Words Spoken By Buddha" (Happy Science's basic sutra) for 45 minutes after she died.

This is the modern version of the raising of Lazarus from death in Christianity. Everyone in the village knew that the girl had been dead for 45 minutes but witnessed her life being restored after the 45-minute recitation of the English sutra, "The True Words Spoken By Buddha." On seeing this, many villagers became Happy Science members. Such a story was introduced in the movie.

I think their faith is pure and straightforward. In a hospital in Japan, it would be almost impossible to revive someone even if you recited "The True Words Spoken By Buddha." Once he or she is pronounced dead, the person would be moved to the mortuary. But even in this day and age, there is someone who came back to life simply because the father recited "The True Words Spoken By Buddha" for 45 minutes.

In Christianity, other than the resurrection of Jesus himself after the crucifixion, the story of the raising of Lazarus is the only miracle that involves resurrecting the dead. So this is one of the greatest miracles. The same kind of resurrection happened when a Happy Science believer in Africa—who is not even a staff member—recited "The True Words Spoken By Buddha." This was because he strongly prayed to El Cantare while reciting it. When he recited the prayer with a strong belief that miracles could happen, the heart of his child began to beat again, and she came back to life. She now goes to school and lives a normal life. Thus, what is considered impossible has actually occurred.

Happy Science has great hidden power as a religion

Some of you may have watched this movie already. In fact, miracles similar to the stories in the movie are happening all around Japan and the world. Yet this is merely the beginning. When faith truly prevails all over the world, even greater miracles will happen.

Even Jesus Christ of Christianity, which is said to have two billion believers in the world, is just another guiding spirit of Happy Science. When you discover this truth, you will understand how great is the hidden power that Happy Science has as a religion.

From now on, we will see, hear, and feel more unexpected things than we ever imagined. And while we are alive in this world, many things that we believe impossible in this world will begin to happen.

The majority of people have been brainwashed by modern education, mass media, and the opinions of their neighbors and are living without knowing their real power or the real power of God and Buddha in the heavenly world. So, from now on, I intend to show you the True World.

The power of natural disasters and catastrophes surmounts human thinking

The year 2020 was said to be the beginning of the Golden Age. So why did we start with the coronavirus pandemic that spread all over the world?

In Japan, there was also heavy flooding due to downpours in Kumamoto Prefecture in the Kyushu region. It affected many places in Kyushu, and dozens of people were killed and tens of thousands were affected. People may have been astounded by the news reports in Japan.

China, our neighbor, also suffers large floods, though they rarely report on them. There were over 70 million casualties due to heavy rain. This is an astonishing number.

People in the affected areas may have started to gradually notice what these disasters might mean. Please know that natural disasters and catastrophes have the power to surmount all boundaries and safeguards created through arrogant human thinking.

For example, Kumamoto Prefecture has experienced many natural disasters, but that is probably because people believed the water level of the river would not increase so much. However, the news reported that the water level of the river reached nine meters (about 30 feet) in height. Because this was a river and not the sea, it may have been natural to believe that the water levels would not get so high; it would be high enough to flood houses. Nevertheless, such a thing happened.

So even if Japan has been taking many different measures to promote initiatives for building national resilience, there will be more natural disasters that nullify those endeavors one after another. This is something I have already predicted. Many typhoons hit Japan in the fall of 2019, and other countries have also suffered similar damages.

The reason the desert locusts are causing damage to various places

What is more, there was an outbreak of desert locusts in East Africa, mainly around Kenya. They spread in Africa, moved to Asia, and even entered Pakistan and India; they ravaged crops wherever they went. In China, both locusts and grasshoppers independently emerged and were ravaging various kinds of crops.

These desert locusts are capable of flying a distance of 150 kilometers (about 93 miles) just by eating two grams of grass a day. This is incredible. Their energy-generating capacity is like that of uranium or atomic energy. Would you be able to fly 150 kilometers with only two grams of grass? It would be impossible for humans to do such a thing. Flying 150 kilometers on only two grams of grass is already amazing, but they do so while producing offspring. They continue to increase in number in this way, and trillions of them fly in swarms.

These locusts have emerged in South America as well and are causing a food crisis. The people there are suffering not only from the spread of the coronavirus but also from the outbreak of locusts.

Many natural disasters resembling the plagues caused by God's wrath in the Book of Exodus in Moses' time are now occurring. The reason why they occur concurrently is a secret for the time being. However, it is not a complete secret, so some of you may have a slight understanding of the possible reasons. Perhaps the natural phenomena are a warning that says, "Human beings are slacking off at a time when El Cantare has descended!" I try not to say this too much because I may sound like a god of vengeance if I do. Some divine punishments will occur, but I intend to bring greater salvation to the world as well.

The meaning of true salvation and true happiness and unhappiness

What I mean by salvation is not confined to the salvation in this world; the salvation in this world is only temporary and not ultimate. Ultimate salvation is to make sure that the people living in this world return to the heavenly world after they die. If a large number of people live in the wrong way and fall to hell after death, it means there was no salvation. Even if such people's illnesses were cured for one year, it does not mean that they were saved.

Ultimately, here is what I want people to know. Humans are spiritual beings; we have souls. The Real World, or the spiritual heavenly world, truly exists, and beings like bodhisattvas and angels as well as higher beings known as God and Buddha are there to watch over this world. We were born on earth from that world, bearing some kind of work or mission to fulfill. We actually carry out work in different occupations, trying to create utopia in this world.

However, everyone is equal before death and we all die one day. This is an unchangeable fact. So dying itself is not unhappiness.

Unhappiness means dying without accomplishing anything.

Unhappiness means dying after making other people unhappy.

Unhappiness means dying without making other people happy.

Unhappiness means dying without guiding others to the Truth.

I want you to change how you think of happiness and unhappiness in this way. For example, having a happy family for several decades in a limited life on earth is a truly small happiness. To be born into this world is very difficult; it is not easy to be born into this world, grow to be an adult with the help of your parents, and work in society. Therefore, if you are blessed with good health and a job others would envy, it means you are carrying a big obligation accordingly. You need to know that you have a duty to guide a large number of people to happiness.

3

How to Overcome Economic Depression

The happiness in our daily lives amidst the coronavirus pandemic

During the months of the coronavirus pandemic, you have probably seen sights you had never seen before and experienced things you had never experienced before. But I do not think they were all bad. By experiencing these hardships, you may have realized that the things you had taken for granted were in fact not guaranteed.

For example, some people may have taken work for granted and disliked getting up every morning, wearing a tie, and going to their company. But when they were told that 80 percent of the employees must stay at home, it must have come as a surprise. Some may have felt anxious, wondering, "What would happen if they tell me they no longer need me while I'm staying at home?" Before this, they may have felt like their salary was guaranteed as long as they went to work, sat at their desk, and secured their position there. But now they were being told not to come to the office and to work remotely instead. If there is no work that can be done from home, it most likely means they will lose their job.

In some large companies, only part-time workers are going to the office while the full-time employees are told to work remotely from home. The full-time workers may fear what would happen in the future. Those who have secured a desk at the office would be more likely to survive at work, so workers in large companies probably feel very insecure about their future.

Many other things that we have never thought about are occurring. We are told, for example, "Keep social distancing," "Don't go outside," "Don't let your children play in the parks," "Don't go shopping every day or don't shop to stroll around with your family. Shop only once every three days." We hear many things we have never heard of before.

In the past, I have mentioned that modern economics and democracy would collapse and that even the military would not be able to operate if this were to continue. If we are not allowed to be in closed spaces, we will not be able to use ships and airplanes. Because close contact is inevitable in the military, the military could not be utilized either. The presidential election campaign recently took place in the U.S., but it should have been canceled if people are not allowed to meet each other. If things continue as they are, the only society possible in the future would be one where people can contact each other only through some kind of device, much like a future society depicted in some movies.

This means we are now being given an opportunity to think and reflect. You can realize, for example, how wonderful it is to be able to work and interact with others; how great it is to be able to let your children play in the park; how blessed you are to be able to go to work even in a packed train, though you may have disliked it; and how fortunate you are to be able to receive a salary even when you are not being productive. Some housewives may have felt bored of not having anything special to do other than to go shopping every day, but they may now realize how happy they were to be able to go shopping every day.

A major economic depression is likely to happen

Although there are no legal laws on self-restraint in Japan, upon the government's request, many shops started to close one after another without knowing when they can reopen. When I walked around to look at the situation, some shops were open despite the government's request. It must have taken courage for them to do so. Certain restaurants, cafes, and shops were open, but they were nervously carrying on their businesses. They were working as they feared being accused of opening their stores. A terrible age has come; people are being accused of working.

The government tells people not to work, but when asked what to do, they only tell people, "We'll think of some measures later." National and local governments say that they might give out money, but even if people receive money, it is clear they will eventually lose their businesses if they keep their shops closed.

Some people have already closed their businesses, but the real disaster has yet to come. Now, people are not as free to travel internationally and various businesses are experiencing "functional paralysis," so a major economic depression is on its way.

The day before I gave this lecture, I traveled to Sohonzan Shoshinkan in Utsunomiya City. On my way there, I changed trains to get on the bullet train at Omiya station. As I was walking on the platform, I saw three kiosks, a kind of convenience store. Two out of the three were closed with a note that read, "Due to the self-restraint orders, we have been closed since March 14." It means they had already been closed for about four months by the time I read the note. The kiosk in the middle was open, but its business hours were from 7:00 a.m. to 1:00 p.m. So, when I got there a little after 1:30 p.m., all the kiosks on the platform were closed.

That is how things were in the fourth month since the self-restraint order was enforced. We can imagine what will happen if this keeps going as it is. Things will no longer be able to return to the way they were.

This made me worry about what might happen if companies like Japan Railways or the major airline companies went bankrupt after creating a deficit of trillions or tens of trillions of yen. Large department stores were also closed for a long time, but there is no way they can survive without selling their goods. Receiving money from the national or local governments would not be enough for them to sustain themselves. There will certainly be many employees who will be fired, and many people will lose their jobs.

As for Happy Science, I am very sorry, but we did not listen to the request of the national or local government and have worked as usual throughout March and onward. Our headquarters are also open as usual. I, too, have been working a little more than usual. In our case, we usually do the opposite of what people believe as common sense.

The importance of restoring the system that allows people to work

In most cases, the trend is already over by the time it becomes a boom in society. But people often do not think about the next step and are too late to act. For example, in Japan, every citizen received a ¥100,000 (about US$1,000) subsidy, and some businesses received ¥300,000, ¥500,000, or ¥1 million as compensation. Some may have already received the money, whereas others are still waiting to hear back about their application. However, rather than distributing money, it is much more important to create an air among the people to think about how to restore the system that will allow them to work again. People are losing to fear, and I have an impression that they are far too weak against the unknown.

Since last spring, almost all weddings have been canceled or postponed in Japan, but if events keep getting pushed back, all companies involved will greatly suffer. There is no need to worry about viruses that are invisible to the eye, and people should push forward with various events such as weddings. In the Japanese calendar, there are days of *taian-kichijitsu* and *butsumetsu* (known as the lucky and unlucky days, respectively). Weddings should be held not only on the days of *taian-kichijitsu* but also on the days of *butsumetsu* because the latter, too, is a wonderful day when Shakyamuni Buddha returned to the heavenly world. So people should hold events without any concerns.

Whenever there is a boom in society, you need to stop for a moment. In most cases, the opposite of what is going on in society is the spiritual way of thinking. It is worth noting that God's way of thinking is often the reverse of what society is thinking about.

Even if you receive a subsidy, it is not of much use right now. Things are slowly starting to reopen, but we are still told not to go shopping or travel so much. We cannot go abroad either. Some people used much of their retirement money to go on a cruise ship, thinking that it would be their last chance to do so, but ended up being trapped inside the ship, like being in a cage, and could not escape being infected by the virus. It is such a fearful world, indeed. So, even if you are given money now, there is not much use for it.

There are also people who have enough money or whose salary did not drop. Public officials did not have their salaries cut, but because they are consuming less, they are investing their money by buying stocks instead. This raised the stock prices, and the value of gold has also marked the highest value ever.

People are investing in various things, but realistically speaking, it is a strange move. Looking at the state of affairs in the world, it is almost certain that a great depression is approaching. Even so, people are buying a lot of stocks. They are continuing to buy stocks when the stocks are likely to become mere pieces of paper soon. Of course, it might be possible to gain some profit if they buy them early and sell them quickly, but objectively speaking, it is foolish to buy stocks when a great depression is coming.

Currently, bank deposits yield almost no interests, and there is talk that bank accounts might be blocked. So people may be in fear that their money could disappear if they left it in the banks. This actually happened once in the late 90s. Japanese people experienced the fear of money disappearing from their bank accounts during the financial crisis in the late 90s.

The fundamental "cure" is to work properly

This is a battle. The fundamental "cure" is to be brave and start working again properly. There is no other way. It is useless to scatter "pieces of paper." Giving out banknotes will not fix anything.

According to Article 5 in the Public Financial Act, the Bank of Japan must not directly purchase government bonds. But there is an exception: Under special circumstances, this law can be overridden. So, in the current circumstances, the Bank of Japan is directly purchasing a lot of government bonds that other banks cannot buy.

What does this imply? The Bank of Japan prints ¥10,000 bills for ¥20–25 each and circulates them as cash that is worth ¥10,000. They are also directly buying bonds issued by the government, which has as much as ¥1,100–1,200 trillion (about US$11–12 trillion) in debt. This means the Bank of Japan will also be "doomed" if these bonds turn into worthless pieces of paper. The chances of this happening are getting higher. But if it truly happens, there will be a huge problem from a macroeconomic perspective.

What remains untouched now is personal savings and corporate internal reserves, so I am afraid the government is thinking of imposing a new tax on them. Although Japanese citizens may be happily receiving the money scattered by the government now, they will eventually have to withstand the tax hike that is coming next.

The importance of perceiving your own mission

After all, these measures alone are not enough to fight through this battle, so we must quickly get back on track and return to our usual work mode. It means we must overcome our fears and fight.

We need to return to the starting point. Illnesses and accidents have existed from a long time. Natural disasters, catastrophes, torrential rains, floods, tsunamis, earthquakes, and fires—these have all existed from a long ago, so we must learn to live with them. Regardless of whether Mt. Fuji erupts or not, human activities must continue.

So, do not sit and wait for a panacea, but instead change your lifestyle so you can live every day to the fullest. It is important to pray to God or Buddha, and while doing so, focus your energy on work that will be a positive influence on the world and will help build a happy future in your afterlife.

No matter how hard we resist, we will all have to leave this world one day. Therefore, just as the lyrics of the songs in the movie *Twiceborn* suggest, we must go with ourselves; even if we make an enemy of the whole world, there are things we must still do.

It is important to perceive your own mission. There must be something that makes you feel, "I was born to do this in this lifetime." Everyone must find this "something" and be determined to fulfill it.

4

Build a Pillar of Faith in You and Realize a Prosperous Future

Gyoki, Kukai, and Nichiren fought disasters with faith and Dharma power

The theme of this chapter, "Creation from Faith," is very difficult. One of the current problems is that even though there are religious beliefs in many developed countries, the contents of their religions or the contents of their faiths are being lost.

When it comes to Japan, it is unclear whether faith exists or not. Japan is adrift and seems like it could easily become a country like North Korea and China. Therefore, a strong pillar of faith must be established in Japan. If Japan since the Meiji Era (after 1868) has not been good enough, we must establish a religion with an even stronger faith—a religion with real faith. It is important to clearly understand the way humans should live, and do work and build relationships with others based on that.

When various diseases prevailed during the Nara Period (in the eighth century) in Japan, the Buddhist monk Gyoki built the Great Buddha statue of Nara. The construction is said to have cost twice the national budget at the time—about ¥200 trillion (about US$2 trillion) today. He managed to collect that much money from the general public. This means that the Buddhist monks had much virtue in those days. Because the government at the time could not collect such a large amount of money, they asked Gyoki to collect the funds. They even asked him to arrange everything that was necessary to build the statue, including schedule management and mobilizing people who could help.

Gyoki was once oppressed by the country in his early years but gained a good reputation later in his life. That is why the government at the time asked him to help build the Great Buddha statue of Nara. Soon after it was built, various diseases and other problems were said to have disappeared.

Kobo Daishi Kukai is another well-known Buddhist monk. When I gave this lecture, we were in the middle of shooting the movie *Beautiful Lure—A Modern Tale of "Painted Skin,"* a story that is related to Kukai.

During the time when Kukai was alive, there was an outbreak of grasshoppers in Japan, which ruined the crops. It caused significant problems, so Kukai was asked to exorcise them. Kukai built a proper altar used in Esoteric Buddhism called *Gomadan*, sat on top of it, and prayed. Then the next day, all of the grasshoppers were said to have disappeared. This story has been historically documented. The fact that grasshoppers completely disappeared in a day shows that even the founder of one school of Buddhism—Japanese Esoteric Buddhism—had enough power to vanish a swarm of grasshoppers.

The Buddhist monk Nichiren is another example. When people were struggling because of drought, he made the rainfall occur by conducting rituals and prayers for rain. In the past, these were all monks' jobs. They were able to bring or stop rainfall. They could even make an outbreak of grasshoppers disappear.

In this way, religion has a much stronger power than you think. In an age when people have strong faith, someone with Dharma power will appear. Such a person is granted the power to fight various problems.

The descent of El Cantare must be taught worldwide

Please tell the entire world that El Cantare is born. If more and more people in the world know of this fact while they are alive, the world will become a much better place. At the very least, I want to eliminate all wars that arise due to religious conflicts, and I believe we can dispel a lot of unknown diseases and natural disasters.

Many people believe that the heavy rainfall and the large-scale locust outbreak are all caused by global warming, but that is not true. The Earth used to be much warmer in the past, but none of these phenomena occurred. They will not happen even if the Earth's temperatures were to rise by 3 or 4°C, so there is no need to worry. The Earth has been through much hotter periods as well as much colder ones.

Humans once lived in an age when lava was still flowing, and we have lived through the Ice Age, too. You may think it is impossible for humans to survive through the Ice Age, but we had the wisdom to survive such a time. That is why humanity continues to survive to this day. So, come what may, have faith in God and overcome any age of hardship.

Put faith first and create a future utopia based on faith

Our souls have lived for a far greater amount of time than you can imagine. Your soul is essentially a Light that branched off from God. This is the fundamental truth. Although your soul may only be a small piece of God's Light, this piece of Light can exert great power if it is polished. Because I approve of this Truth, I continue to support democracy without denying it.

In other words, if you polish your Buddha-nature with the awareness of being the child of God or Buddha, it will surely bloom and you will be able to attain a certain level of enlightenment. This is the same principle as democracy.

So each of you must be aware that you have Buddha-nature and must carry out your activities while constantly examining whether you are right or wrong based on God's Will. If all of us adopt such attitudes and make efforts to establish good politics in this world, we can surely create a future utopia and ideal political and economic systems of the future.

But to make this happen, we must put faith first and firmly believe in God. Everything must start from faith. Only when there is supremacy of faith can there be political prosperity, economic prosperity, advancement in science and technology, and other cultural prosperity centered around religion. We must not deviate from this central axis.

Currently, there are barely any political parties and politicians that say this. Those who do business activities based on economic principles do not think like this either, and they only judge things based on whether something can make them money or not. There is no way of telling apart good money from the bad in modern economics. For this reason, some people think they can do whatever they want to do as long as it is not regarded as a crime. But that cannot be, for there is certainly good money and bad money.

Good money is money that was earned from working hard to bring the world closer to utopia. This is how I would like you to work as well.

There are people who have mobility problems due to age and people who cannot work due to a disability or illness, so it is also important to reach out to help these people. I believe it is one of our obligations. However, if you have a healthy body and a healthy mind, please try to be more diligent and be determined to say, "I'm going to bring down God's glory on earth. I'm going to succeed even more and make this world shine brighter." Although helping underprivileged people with such virtuous thoughts is important, it is impossible for everyone to quit his or her job and live on cash handouts from the government. Please know that this is not possible.

You can stay young as long as you hold on to your ideals

Even if you retire from work after reaching a certain age, it does not mean that your work in this world has finished in the truest sense. Praying in your mind is also work. To offer advice to other people is also work. You can give advice to young people even when you are 90 years old. If it is about a religious matter, there is so much guidance you can give.

Work that generates profit is not the only work there is. Even if you can no longer make money, there is still work to do. Please know that there is still potential for your work to develop and expand further according to your age.

As for me, if I were working in a regular company, I would already be retired at my age. But I still look like I am about 40 years old. This means people should not judge themselves based on their physical age. If you continue to receive God's Light from the heavenly world as "fuel," youth will be yours forever and you will be able to keep on working.

People age when they lose their ideals. If you hold on to your ideals, you can keep on living in youth.

I have already given over 3,250 lectures (as of February 2021), but I will continue onward. So please follow me.

I do not wish for only young people to stay with me and for people over 60 years of age to go away. To the owners of *Daikokuten* (Angel of Wealth) businesses supporting Happy Science, I would like to say, "No matter what may come, be it viruses, floods, or locusts, don't let them defeat you!" Please be resolute and think, "I will prosper even if I make an enemy of the whole world."

Happy Science has greater potential than this. Right now, we can hardly say we are at the half-way point to our destination. I cannot die yet while we are still at such a level. We must be 10 times or 100 times greater than we are now. At this point, we will be remembered as the largest religion in Japan to have developed after World War II but nothing more than that. We must be known across the whole world.

Be a person who can give hope and courage to others

The day before I gave this lecture, I watched the movie *Cinderella Man*, which I had watched more than once. It is a story about a man in New York who loses his job as a boxer during the Great Depression in 1929 but makes a comeback later to become the world champion.

Just like in the movie, we need hope. We need someone who can give courage. Even if a worldwide depression were to occur, there needs to be someone who can give hope and courage to others at that time.

When there is someone who is working hard or a company that is trying hard to survive, others can also regain hope and courage and can stand back up again. So, much like the main character in the movie, who trained his left hand after breaking his right hand and used his left punches to win back the championship, it is important to have resilience.

Do not use your current environment or condition as an excuse. Instead, let us build up a new power and use that power to lead the world.

I say to the people of the world.

Happy Science activities are centered in Japan right now, so it goes without saying that Japan needs to become a stronger nation. But I also want other countries, like the U.S., to pull through and not let the coronavirus pandemic slow them down or cause them to lose momentum.

Furthermore, we have recently been critical of China, but we do not see it as a battle between the 7 million people in Hong Kong versus the 1.4 billion people of mainland China; we do not think that the 7 million people should live while the 1.4 billion people die. We are simply trying to encourage them to think about which way of life makes people happy and to choose that way of life.

We criticize China now but only as a temporary means to guide them. We intend to ultimately lead China and all other countries to develop and prosper. So please do not forget your love for humanity.

May you have more power!

More Light!

And more prosperity!

If the God you believe in is the true God, the future of prosperity shall open before you. I pray for this to come true from the bottom of my heart.

Afterword

One special feature of this book is the truth that we coexist with spiritual influences as we live in this world. If we live without realizing this truth, it will be as if we are walking around the room with sunglasses on.

There was a woman who lost some of her hair and developed several bald spots after becoming the target of another woman's envy. But when I identified the *ikiryo* (spirit of a living person) possessing her and commanded it to leave, her hair grew back rapidly in just one to two months. This may sound like a story from the Heian Era,[3] but it is simply because people today have forgotten Buddha's Truth.

This book describes the ways to conquer the devils as well as how to dispel viruses. It also reveals the mystical power of God and the miraculous power of faith. I believe people today need to learn this Truth afresh as a new subject of study.

This will definitely be a life-changing book for you.

Ryuho Okawa
Master & CEO of Happy Science Group
December 2020

TRANSLATOR'S NOTE

1 Heaven also consists of the front side and the rear side, and the rear side of heaven is inhabited by *tengu*, *sennin*, *yokai*, and *youko*. Refer to *The Laws of the Sun* (New York: IRH Press, 2018).

2 *The Real Exorcist* and *How to Create the Spiritual Screen* are available at Happy Science.

3 In the Heian Era (794–1185), *Onmyoji* (Yin-Yang Masters) were active in dispelling malicious spirits.

This book is a compilation of the lectures, with additions, as listed below.

- Chapter One -

The Secret World of Religion

Unveiling the Truth about This World and the Afterworld

Japanese title: *Shukyo no Himitsu no Sekai*
Lecture given on February 2, 2020,
at the Special Lecture Hall of Happy Science, Japan

- Chapter Two -

Recovering from Spiritual Disturbance

Secrets about the Viral Infection and Spiritual Possession

Japanese title: *Reishosha no Tachinaori ni tsuite*
Lecture given on March 28, 2020,
at the Special Lecture Hall of Happy Science, Japan

- Chapter Three -

The Condition of the Real Exorcist

The Spiritual Initiation on Exorcism

Japanese title: *The Real Exorcist no Joken*
Lecture given on February 6, 2020,
at the Special Lecture Hall of Happy Science, Japan

- Chapter Four -

The Right Way to Conquer the Devils

Spiritual Power to Make the World Brighter

Japanese title: *Gouma no Hondo*
Lecture given on October 4, 2020,
at Holy Land El Cantare Seitankan of Happy Science,
Tokushima Prefecture, Japan

- Chapter Five -

Creation from Faith

Secrets to Overcoming the Crisis Humanity Faces

Japanese title: *Shinko karano Souzo*
Lecture given on July 12, 2020,
at Head Temple Sohonzan Shoshinkan of Happy Science,
Tochigi Prefecture, Japan

ABOUT THE AUTHOR

RYUHO OKAWA was born on July 7th 1956, in Tokushima, Japan. After graduating from the University of Tokyo with a law degree, he joined a Tokyo-based trading house. While working at its New York headquarters, he studied international finance at the Graduate Center of the City University of New York. In 1981, he attained Great Enlightenment and became aware that he is El Cantare with a mission to bring salvation to all humankind. In 1986, he established Happy Science. It now has members in over 160 countries across the world, with more than 700 local branches and temples as well as 10,000 missionary houses around the world. The total number of lectures has exceeded 3,300 (of which more than 150 are in English) and over 2,850 books (of which more than 600 are Spiritual Interview Series) have been published, many of which are translated into 37 languages. Many of the books, including *The Laws of the Sun* have become best sellers or million sellers. To date, Happy Science has produced 23 movies. The original story and original concept were given by the Executive Producer Ryuho Okawa. Recent movie titles are *Beautiful Lure–A Modern Tale of "Painted Skin"* (live-action, May 2021), *Into the Dreams…and Horror Experiences* (live-action, August 2021), and *The Laws of the Universe–The Age of Elohim* (animation movie scheduled to be released in October 2021). He has also composed the lyrics and music of over 450 songs, such as theme songs and featured songs of movies. Moreover, he is the Founder of Happy Science University and Happy Science Academy (Junior and Senior High School), Founder and President of the Happiness Realization Party, Founder and Honorary Headmaster of Happy Science Institute of Government and Management, Founder of IRH Press Co., Ltd., and the Chairperson of NEW STAR PRODUCTION Co., Ltd. and ARI Production Co., Ltd.

WHAT IS EL CANTARE?

El Cantare means "the Light of the Earth," and is the Supreme God of the Earth who has been guiding humankind since the beginning of Genesis. He is whom Jesus called Father and Muhammad called Allah. Different parts of El Cantare's core consciousness have descended to Earth in the past, once as Alpha and another as Elohim. His branch spirits, such as Shakyamuni Buddha and Hermes, have descended to Earth many times and helped to flourish many civilizations. To unite various religions and to integrate various fields of study in order to build a new civilization on Earth, a part of the core consciousness has descended to Earth as Master Ryuho Okawa.

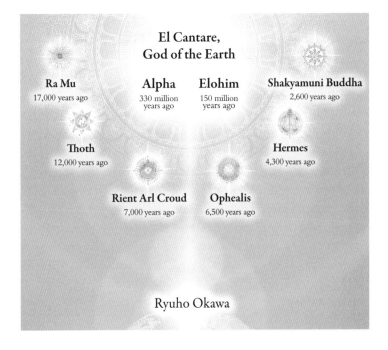

**El Cantare,
God of the Earth**

Ra Mu
17,000 years ago

Alpha
330 million
years ago

Elohim
150 million
years ago

Shakyamuni Buddha
2,600 years ago

Thoth
12,000 years ago

Hermes
4,300 years ago

Rient Arl Croud
7,000 years ago

Ophealis
6,500 years ago

Ryuho Okawa

Alpha is a part of the core consciousness of El Cantare who descended to Earth around 330 million years ago. Alpha preached Earth's Truths to harmonize and unify Earth-born humans and space people who came from other planets.

Elohim is a part of El Cantare's core consciousness who descended to Earth around 150 million years ago. He gave wisdom, mainly on the differences of light and darkness, good and evil.

Shakyamuni Buddha was born as a prince into the Shakya Clan in India around 2,600 years ago. When he was 29 years old, he renounced the world and sought enlightenment. He later attained Great Enlightenment and founded Buddhism.

Hermes is one of the 12 Olympian gods in Greek mythology, but the spiritual Truth is that he taught the teachings of love and progress around 4,300 years ago that became the origin of the current Western civilization. He is a hero that truly existed.

Ophealis was born in Greece around 6,500 years ago and was the leader who took an expedition to as far as Egypt. He is the God of miracles, prosperity, and arts, and is known as Osiris in the Egyptian mythology.

Rient Arl Croud was born as a king of the ancient Incan Empire around 7,000 years ago and taught about the mysteries of the mind. In the heavenly world, he is responsible for the interactions that take place between various planets.

Thoth was an almighty leader who built the golden age of the Atlantic civilization around 12,000 years ago. In the Egyptian mythology, he is known as god Thoth.

Ra Mu was a leader who built the golden age of the civilization of Mu around 17,000 years ago. As a religious leader and a politician, he ruled by uniting religion and politics.

ABOUT HAPPY SCIENCE

Happy Science is a global movement that empowers individuals to find purpose and spiritual happiness and to share that happiness with their families, societies, and the world. With more than 12 million members around the world, Happy Science aims to increase awareness of spiritual truths and expand our capacity for love, compassion, and joy so that together we can create the kind of world we all wish to live in.

Activities at Happy Science are based on the Principles of Happiness (Love, Wisdom, Self-Reflection, and Progress). These principles embrace worldwide philosophies and beliefs, transcending boundaries of culture and religions.

Love teaches us to give ourselves freely without expecting anything in return; it encompasses giving, nurturing, and forgiving.

Wisdom leads us to the insights of spiritual truths, and opens us to the true meaning of life and the will of God (the universe, the highest power, Buddha).

Self-Reflection brings a mindful, nonjudgmental lens to our thoughts and actions to help us find our truest selves—the essence of our souls—and deepen our connection to the highest power. It helps us attain a clean and peaceful mind and leads us to the right life path.

Progress emphasizes the positive, dynamic aspects of our spiritual growth—actions we can take to manifest and spread happiness around the world. It's a path that not only expands our soul growth, but also furthers the collective potential of the world we live in.

PROGRAMS AND EVENTS

The doors of Happy Science are open to all. We offer a variety of programs and events, including self-exploration and self-growth programs, spiritual seminars, meditation and contemplation sessions, study groups, and book events.

Our programs are designed to:
* Deepen your understanding of your purpose and meaning in life
* Improve your relationships and increase your capacity to love unconditionally
* Attain peace of mind, decrease anxiety and stress, and feel positive
* Gain deeper insights and a broader perspective on the world
* Learn how to overcome life's challenges
  ... and much more.

*For more information, visit **happy-science.org**.*

CONTACT INFORMATION

Happy Science is a worldwide organization with faith centers around the globe. For a comprehensive list of centers, visit the worldwide directory at *happy-science.org*. The following are some of the many Happy Science locations:

UNITED STATES AND CANADA

New York
79 Franklin St., New York, NY 10013
Phone: 212-343-7972
Fax: 212-343-7973
Email: ny@happy-science.org
Website: happyscience-usa.org

Los Angeles
1590 E. Del Mar Blvd., Pasadena, CA 91106
Phone: 626-395-7775
Fax: 626-395-7776
Email: la@happy-science.org
Website: happyscience-usa.org

New Jersey
725 River Rd, #102B, Edgewater, NJ 07020
Phone: 201-313-0127
Fax: 201-313-0120
Email: nj@happy-science.org
Website: happyscience-usa.org

Orange County
10231 Slater Ave., #204
Fountain Valley, CA 92708
Phone: 714-659-1501
Email: oc@happy-science.org
Website: happyscience-usa.org

Florida
5208 8th St., St. Zephyrhills, FL 33542
Phone: 813-715-0000
Fax: 813-715-0010
Email: florida@happy-science.org
Website: happyscience-usa.org

San Diego
7841 Balboa Ave., Suite #202
San Diego, CA 92111
Phone: 626-395-7775
Fax: 626-395-7776
E-mail: sandiego@happy-science.org
Website: happyscience-usa.org

Atlanta
1874 Piedmont Ave., NE Suite 360-C
Atlanta, GA 30324
Phone: 404-892-7770
Email: atlanta@happy-science.org
Website: happyscience-usa.org

Hawaii
Phone: 808-591-9772
Fax: 808-591-9776
Email: hi@happy-science.org
Website: happyscience-usa.org

San Francisco
525 Clinton St.
Redwood City, CA 94062
Phone & Fax: 650-363-2777
Email: sf@happy-science.org
Website: happyscience-usa.org

Kauai
3343 Kanakolu Street, Suite 5
Lihue, HI 96766, U.S.A.
Phone: 808-822-7007
Fax: 808-822-6007
Email: kauai-hi@happy-science.org
Website: happyscience-usa.org

Toronto
845 The Queensway
Etobicoke ON M8Z 1N6 Canada
Phone: 1-416-901-3747
Email: toronto@happy-science.org
Website: happy-science.ca

Vancouver
#201-2607 East 49th Avenue
Vancouver, BC, V5S 1J9, Canada
Phone: 1-604-437-7735
Fax: 1-604-437-7764
Email: vancouver@happy-science.org
Website: happy-science.ca

INTERNATIONAL

Tokyo
1-6-7 Togoshi, Shinagawa
Tokyo, 142-0041 Japan
Phone: 81-3-6384-5770
Fax: 81-3-6384-5776
Email: tokyo@happy-science.org
Website: happy-science.org

Seoul
74, Sadang-ro 27-gil,
Dongjak-gu, Seoul, Korea
Phone: 82-2-3478-8777
Fax: 82-2-3478-9777
Email: korea@happy-science.org
Website: happyscience-korea.org

London
3 Margaret St.
London,W1W 8RE United Kingdom
Phone: 44-20-7323-9255
Fax: 44-20-7323-9344
Email: eu@happy-science.org
Website: happyscience-uk.org

Taipei
No. 89, Lane 155, Dunhua N. Road
Songshan District, Taipei City 105, Taiwan
Phone: 886-2-2719-9377
Fax: 886-2-2719-5570
Email: taiwan@happy-science.org
Website: happyscience-tw.org

Sydney
516 Pacific Hwy, Lane Cove North,
NSW 2066, Australia
Phone: 61-2-9411-2877
Fax: 61-2-9411-2822
Email: sydney@happy-science.org

Malaysia
No 22A, Block 2, Jalil Link Jalan Jalil Jaya 2,
Bukit Jalil 57000, Kuala Lumpur, Malaysia
Phone: 60-3-8998-7877
Fax: 60-3-8998-7977
Email: malaysia@happy-science.org
Website: happyscience.org.my

Brazil Headquarters
Rua. Domingos de Morais 1154,
Vila Mariana, Sao Paulo SP
CEP 04010-100, Brazil
Phone: 55-11-5088-3800
Email: sp@happy-science.org
Website: happyscience.com.br

Nepal
Kathmandu Metropolitan City Ward
No. 15,
Ring Road, Kimdol,
Sitapaila Kathmandu, Nepal
Phone: 97-714-272931
Email: nepal@happy-science.org

Jundiai
Rua Congo, 447, Jd. Bonfiglioli
Jundiai-CEP, 13207-340
Phone: 55-11-4587-5952
Email: jundiai@happy-science.org

Uganda
Plot 877 Rubaga Road, Kampala
P.O. Box 34130, Kampala, Uganda
Phone: 256-79-4682-121
Email: uganda@happy-science.org
Website: happyscience-uganda.org

ABOUT HAPPINESS REALIZATION PARTY

The Happiness Realization Party (HRP) was founded in May 2009 by Master Ryuho Okawa as part of the Happy Science Group to offer concrete and proactive solutions to the current issues such as military threats from North Korea and China and the long-term economic recession. HRP aims to implement drastic reforms of the Japanese government, thereby bringing peace and prosperity to Japan. To accomplish this, HRP proposes two key policies:

1) Strengthening the national security and the Japan-U.S. alliance, which plays a vital role in the stability of Asia.

2) Improving the Japanese economy by implementing drastic tax cuts, taking monetary easing measures and creating new major industries.

HRP advocates that Japan should offer a model of a religious nation that allows diverse values and beliefs to coexist, and that contributes to global peace.

*For more information, visit **en.hr-party.jp***

HAPPY SCIENCE ACADEMY
JUNIOR AND SENIOR HIGH SCHOOL

Happy Science Academy Junior and Senior High School is a boarding school founded with the goal of educating the future leaders of the world who can have a big vision, persevere, and take on new challenges.

Currently, there are two campuses in Japan; the Nasu Main Campus in Tochigi Prefecture, founded in 2010, and the Kansai Campus in Shiga Prefecture, founded in 2013.

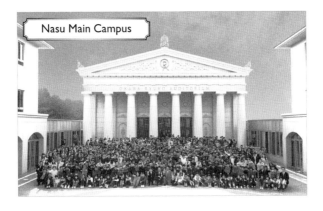

Nasu Main Campus

Kansai Campus

HAPPY SCIENCE UNIVERSITY

THE FOUNDING SPIRIT AND THE GOAL OF EDUCATION

Based on the founding philosophy of the university, "Exploration of happiness and the creation of a new civilization," education, research and studies will be provided to help students acquire deep understanding grounded in religious belief and advanced expertise with the objectives of producing "great talents of virtue" who can contribute in a broad-ranging way to serve Japan and the international society.

FACULTIES

Faculty of human happiness

Students in this faculty will pursue liberal arts from various perspectives with a multidisciplinary approach, explore and envision an ideal state of human beings and society.

Faculty of successful management

This faculty aims to realize successful management that helps organizations to create value and wealth for society and to contribute to the happiness and the development of management and employees as well as society as a whole.

Faculty of future creation

Students in this faculty study subjects such as political science, journalism, performing arts and artistic expression, and explore and present new political and cultural models based on truth, goodness and beauty.

Faculty of future industry

This faculty aims to nurture engineers who can resolve various issues facing modern civilization from a technological standpoint and contribute to the creation of new industries of the future.

ABOUT IRH PRESS USA

IRH Press USA Inc. was founded in 2013 as an affiliated firm of IRH Press Co., Ltd. Based in New York, the press publishes books in various categories including spirituality, religion, and self-improvement and publishes books by Ryuho Okawa, the author of over 100 million books sold worldwide. For more information, visit *okawabooks.com*.

Follow us on:

Facebook: Okawa Books   **Twitter**: Okawa Books

Goodreads: Ryuho Okawa   **Instagram**: OkawaBooks

Pinterest: Okawa Books

NEWSLETTER

To receive book related news, promotions and events, please subscribe to our newsletter below.

 https://okawabooks.us11.list-manage.com/subscribe?u=1fc70960eefd92668052ab7f8&id=2fbd8150ef

MEDIA

OKAWA BOOK CLUB

 A conversation about Ryuho Okawa's titles, topics ranging from self-help, current affairs, spirituality and religions.

Available at iTunes, Spotify and Amazon Music.

 Apple iTunes:
https://podcasts.apple.com/us/podcast/okawa-book-club/id1527893043

 Spotify:
https://open.spotify.com/show/09mpgX2iJ6stVm4eBRdo2b

 Amazon Music:
https://music.amazon.com/podcasts/7b759f24-ff72-4523-bfee-24f48294998f/Okawa-Book-Club

BOOKS BY RYUHO OKAWA

RYUHO OKAWA'S LAWS SERIES

The Laws Series is an annual volume of books that are mainly comprised of Ryuho Okawa's lectures on various topics that highlight principles and guidelines for the activities of Happy Science every year. *The Laws of the Sun*, the first publication of the laws series, ranked in the annual best-selling list in Japan in 1987. Since then, all of the laws series' titles have ranked in the annual best-selling list for more than two decades, setting socio-cultural trends in Japan and around the world.

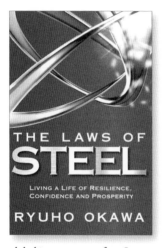

The 26th Laws Series

THE LAWS OF STEEL

LIVING A LIFE OF RESILIENCE, CONFIDENCE AND PROSPERITY

Paperback • 256 pages • $16.95
ISBN: 978-1-942125-65-5

This book is a compilation of six lectures that Ryuho Okawa gave in 2018 and 2019, each containing passionate messages for us to open a brighter future. This powerful and inspiring book will not only show us the ways to achieve true happiness and prosperity, but also the ways to solve many global issues we now face. It presents us with wisdom that is based on a spiritual perspective, and a new design for our future society. Through this book, we can overcome differences in values and create a peaceful world, thereby ushering in a Golden Age.

*For a complete list of books, visit **okawabooks.com***

THE TRILOGY

The first three volumes of the Laws Series, *The Laws of the Sun*, *The Golden Laws*, and *The Nine Dimensions* make a trilogy that completes the basic framework of the teachings of God's Truths. *The Laws of the Sun* discusses the structure of God's Laws, *The Golden Laws* expounds on the doctrine of time, and *The Nine Dimensions* reveals the nature of space.

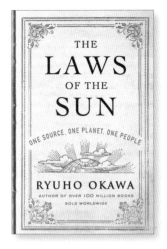

THE LAWS OF THE SUN

ONE SOURCE, ONE PLANET, ONE PEOPLE

Paperback • 288 pages • $15.95
ISBN: 978-1-942125-43-3

IMAGINE IF YOU COULD ASK GOD why He created this world and what spiritual laws He used to shape us—and everything around us. If we could understand His designs and intentions, we could discover what our goals in life should be and whether our actions move us closer to those goals or farther away.

At a young age, a spiritual calling prompted Ryuho Okawa to outline what he innately understood to be universal truths for all humankind. In *The Laws of the Sun*, Okawa outlines these laws of the universe and provides a road map for living one's life with greater purpose and meaning.

In this powerful book, Ryuho Okawa reveals the transcendent nature of consciousness and the secrets of our multidimensional universe and our place in it. By understanding the different stages of love and following the Buddhist Eightfold Path, he believes we can speed up our eternal process of development. *The Laws of the Sun* shows the way to realize true happiness—a happiness that continues from this world through the other.

---

*For a complete list of books, visit **okawabooks.com***

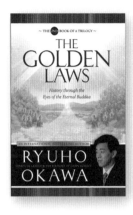

THE GOLDEN LAWS
HISTORY THROUGH THE EYES OF THE ETERNAL BUDDHA

Paperback • 201 pages • $14.95
ISBN: 978-1-941779-81-1

Throughout history, Great Guiding Spirits of Light have been present on Earth in both the East and the West at crucial points in human history to further our spiritual development. *The Golden Laws* reveals how Divine Plan has been unfolding on Earth, and outlines 5,000 years of the secret history of humankind. Once we understand the true course of history, through past, present and into the future, we cannot help but become aware of the significance of our spiritual mission in the present age.

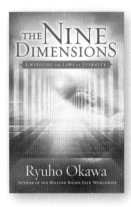

THE NINE DIMENSIONS
UNVEILING THE LAWS OF ETERNITY

Paperback • 168 pages • $15.95
ISBN: 978-0-982698-56-3

This book is a window into the mind of our loving God, who designed this world and the vast, wondrous world of our afterlife as a school with many levels through which our souls learn and grow. When the religions and cultures of the world discover the truth of their common spiritual origin, they will be inspired to accept their differences, come together under faith in God, and build an era of harmony and peaceful progress on Earth.

*For a complete list of books, visit **okawabooks.com***

THE TRUE EIGHTFOLD PATH

GUIDEPOSTS FOR SELF-INNOVATION

Paperback • 272 pages • $16.95
ISBN: 978-1-942125-80-8

This book explains how we can apply the Eightfold Path, one of the main pillars of Shakyamuni Buddha's teachings, as everyday guideposts in the modern-age to achieve self-innovation to live better and make positive changes in these uncertain times.

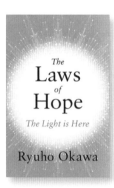

THE LAWS OF HOPE

THE LIGHT IS HERE

Paperback • 224 pages • $16.95
ISBN:978-1-942125-76-1

This book provides ways to bring light and hope to ourselves through our own efforts, even in the midst of sufferings and adversities. Inspired by a wish to bring happiness, success, and hope to humanity, Okawa shows us how to look at and think about our lives and circumstances. By making efforts in your current circumstances, you can fulfill your mission to shed light on yourself and those around you.

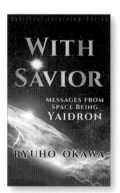

WITH SAVIOR

MESSAGES FROM SPACE BEING YAIDRON

Paperback • 232 pages • $13.95
ISBN: 978-1-943869-94-7

The human race is now faced with multiple unprecedented crises. Perhaps God is warning us humans to reconsider our materialistic and arrogant ways. Fortunately, God has sent us a savior, who is now teaching us to repent and showing us the path we should choose. In this book, space being Yaidron sends his warnings and messages of hope.

---

*For a complete list of books, visit **okawabooks.com***

THE POWER OF BASICS
INTRODUCTION TO MODERN ZEN LIFE OF CALM, SPIRITUALITY AND SUCCESS

Paperback • 232 pages • $16.95
ISBN:978-1-942125-75-4

The power of basics is a necessary asset to excel at any kind of work. It is the power to meticulously pursue tasks with a quiet Zen mindset. If you master this power of basics, you can achieve new levels of productivity regardless of your profession, and attain new heights of success and happiness. This book also describes the essence of an intellectual life, thereby reviving the true spirit of Zen in the modern age.

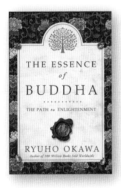

THE ESSENCE OF BUDDHA
THE PATH TO ENLIGHTENMENT

Paperback • 208 pages • $14.95
ISBN: 978-1-942125-06-8

In this book, Ryuho Okawa imparts in simple and accessible language his wisdom about the essence of Shakyamuni Buddha's philosophy of life and enlightenment–teachings that have been inspiring people all over the world for over 2,500 years. By offering a new perspective on core Buddhist thoughts that have long been cloaked in mystique, Okawa brings these teachings to life for modern people. The Essence of Buddha distills a way of life that anyone can practice to achieve a life of self-growth, compassionate living, and true happiness.

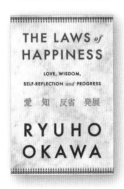

THE LAWS OF HAPPINESS
LOVE, WISDOM, SELF-REFLECTION AND PROGRESS

Paperback • 264 pages • $16.95
ISBN: 978-1-942125-70-9

What is happiness? In this book, Ryuho Okawa explains that happiness is not found outside us; it's found within us, in how we think, how we look at our lives in this world, what we believe in, and how we devote our hearts to the work we do. Even as we go through suffering and unfavorable circumstances, we can always shift our mindset and become happier by simply *giving love* instead of *taking love*.

---

*For a complete list of books, visit **okawabooks.com***

THE REAL EXORCIST

ATTAIN WISDOM TO CONQUER EVIL

Paperback • 208 pages • $16.95
ISBN:978-1-942125-67-9

This is a profound spiritual text backed by the author's nearly 40 years of real-life experience with spiritual phenomena. In it, Okawa teaches how we may discern and overcome our negative tendencies, by acquiring the right knowledge, mindset and lifestyle.

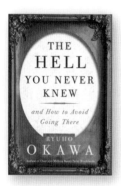

THE HELL YOU NEVER KNEW

AND HOW TO AVOID GOING THERE

Paperback • 192 pages • $15.95
ISBN: 978-1-942125-52-5

From ancient times, people have been warned of the danger of falling to Hell. But does the world of Hell truly exist? If it does, what kind of people would go there? Through his spiritual abilities, Ryuho Okawa found out that Hell is only a small part of the vast Spirit World, yet more than half of the people today go there after they die.

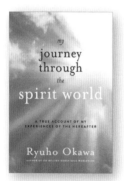

MY JOURNEY THROUGH THE SPIRIT WORLD

A TRUE ACCOUNT OF MY EXPERIENCES OF THE HEREAFTER

Paperback • 224 pages • $15.95
ISBN: 978-1-942125-41-9

In this book, Ryuho Okawa shares surprising facts of the afterworld. This unique and authentic guide to the spirit world will awaken us to the truth of life and death, and show us how we should start living so that we can return to a bright world of heaven.

---

*For a complete list of books, visit **okawabooks.com***

The New Resurrection

My Miraculous Story of Overcoming Illness and Death

Hardcover • 224 pages • $19.95
ISBN: 978-1-942125-64-8

The New Resurrection is an autobiographical account of an astonishing miracle experienced by author Ryuho Okawa in 2004. This event was adapted into the feature-length film *Immortal Hero*, released in Japan, the United States and Canada during the Fall of 2019. Today, Okawa lives each day with the readiness to die for the Truth and has dedicated his life to selflessly guiding faith seekers towards spiritual development and happiness.

Healing from Within

Life-Changing Keys to Calm, Spiritual, and Healthy Living

Paperback • 208 pages • $15.95
ISBN:978-1-942125-18-1

None of us wants to become sick, but why is it that we can't avoid illness in life? Is there a meaning behind illness? In this book, author Ryuho Okawa reveals the true causes and remedies for various illnesses that modern medicine doesn't know how to heal. Building a happier and healthier life starts with believing in the power of our mind and understanding the relationship between mind and body.

Healing Power

The True Mechanism of Mind and Illness

Paperback • 189 pages • $14.95
ISBN: 978-1-941779-96-5

This book clearly describes the relationship between the mind and illness, and provides you with hints to restore your mental and physical health. Cancer, heart disease, allergy, skin disease, dementia, psychiatric disorder, atopy... Many miracles of healing are happening!

---

*For a complete list of books, visit **okawabooks.com***

HOW TO SURVIVE
THE CORONAVIRUS RECESSION

BASICS OF EXORCISM
How to Protect You and Your Family from Evil Spirits

SPIRITUAL WORLD 101
A Guide to a Spiritually Happy Life

THE POSSESSION
Know the Ghost Condition and
Overcome Negative Spiritual Influence

THE MYSTICAL LAWS
Going Beyond the Dimensional Boundaries

THE MIRACLE OF MEDITATION
Opening Your Life to Peace, Joy, and the Power Within

MESSAGES FROM HEAVEN
What Jesus, Buddha, Moses, and Muhammad Would Say Today

THINK BIG!
Be Positive and Be Brave to Achieve Your Dreams

WORRY-FREE LIVING
Let Go of Stress and Live in Peace and Happiness

---

*For a complete list of books, visit **okawabooks.com***

MUSIC BY RYUHO OKAWA

THE THUNDER

a composition for repelling the Coronavirus

We have been granted this music from our Lord. It will repel away the novel Coronavirus originated in China. Experience this magnificent powerful music.

Search on YouTube

the thunder coronavirus 🔍 *for a short ad!*

THE EXORCISM

prayer music for repelling Lost Spirits

Feel the divine vibrations of this Japanese and Western exorcising symphony to banish all evil possessions you suffer from and to purify your space!

Search on YouTube

the exorcism repelling 🔍 *for a short ad!*

 Listen online
Spotify iTunes Amazon

CD available at amazon.com, and Happy Science local branches & shoja (temples)

WITH SAVIOR

English version

"Come what may, you shall expect your future"

This is the message of hope to the modern people who are living in the midst of the Coronavirus pandemic, natural disasters, economic depression, and other various crises.

Search on YouTube | with savior 🔍 | for a short ad!

THE WATER REVOLUTION

English and Chinese version

"Power to the People!"

For the truth and happiness of the 1.4 billion people in China who have no freedom. Love, justice, and sacred rage of God are on this melody that will give you courage to fight to bring peace.

Search on YouTube | the water revolution 🔍 | for a short ad!

CD available at amazon.com, and Happy Science local branches & shoja (temples)

 Listen online
Spotify **iTunes** **Amazon**